Tender Puppies Coloring Book

By Gary Wittmann

Tender Puppies Coloring Book

©By Gary Wittmann

First Published, 2018 by Gary Wittmann
Printed in the United States of America

Check Gary Wittmann on www.garywittmann.com   website.
Facebook 30 Days of Coloring Books for Kids and Adults

Rules to follow:

1. Put a cardboard under where you are coloring. So that the marker doesn't bleed through.
2. Have FUN.
3. Get up to date about new coloring books at

www.getspecialbonus.com/coloringbooks/

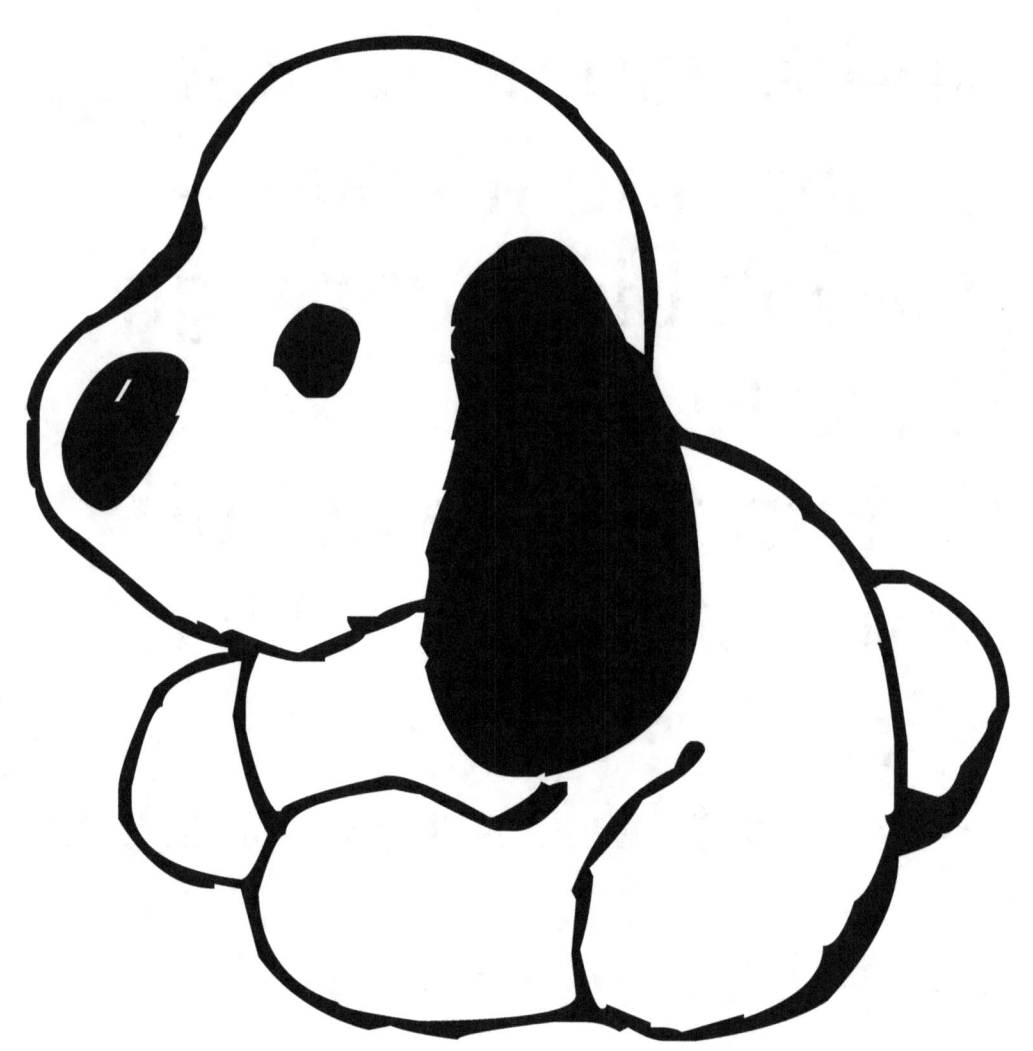

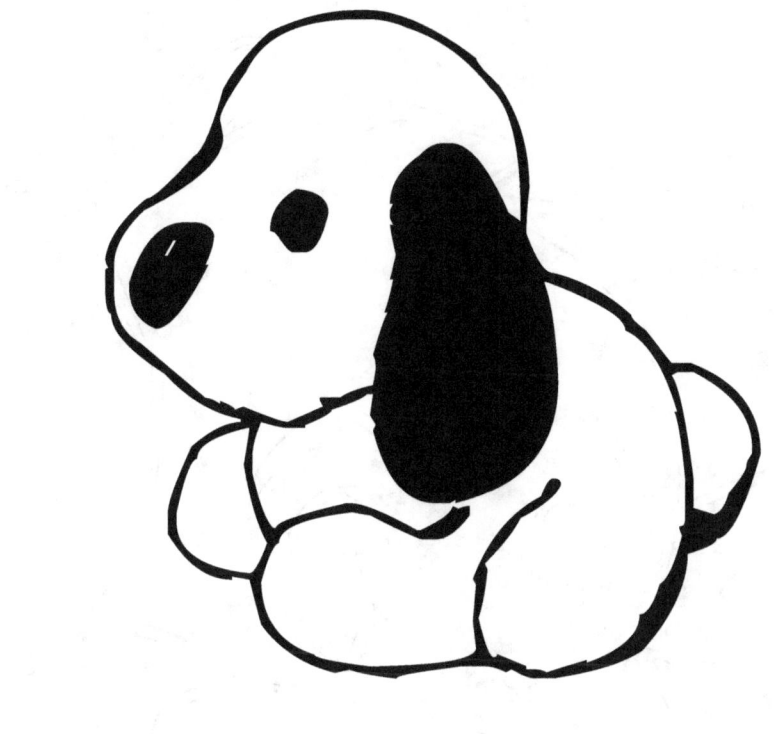

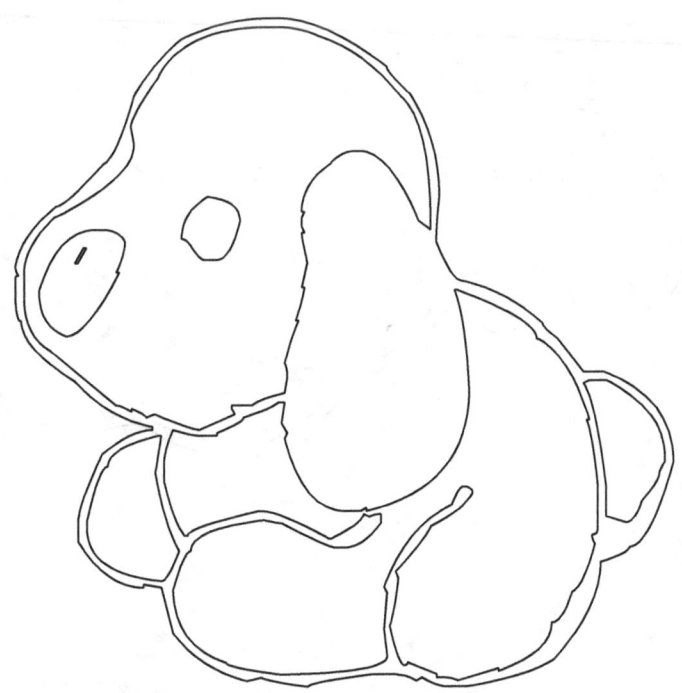

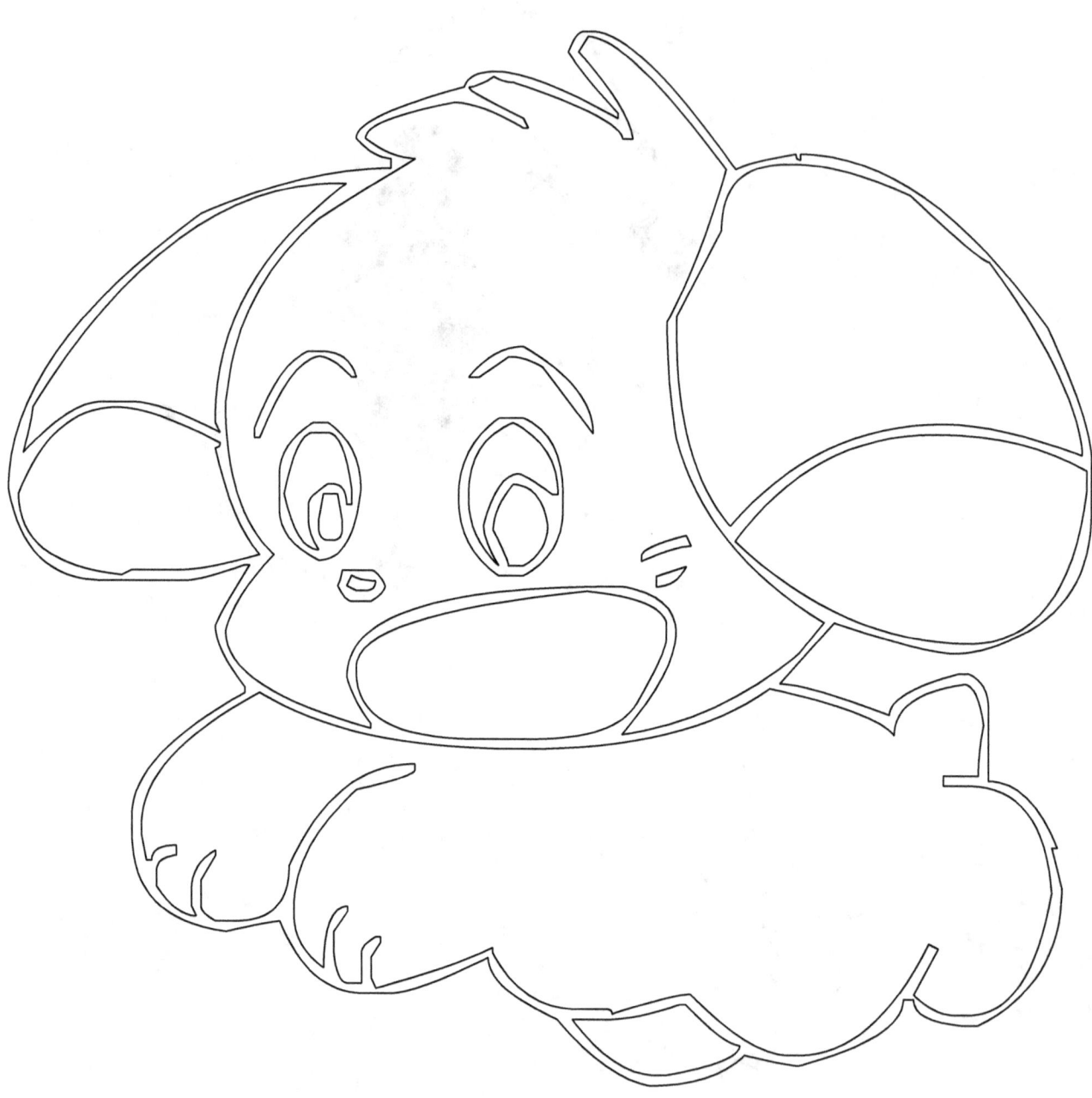

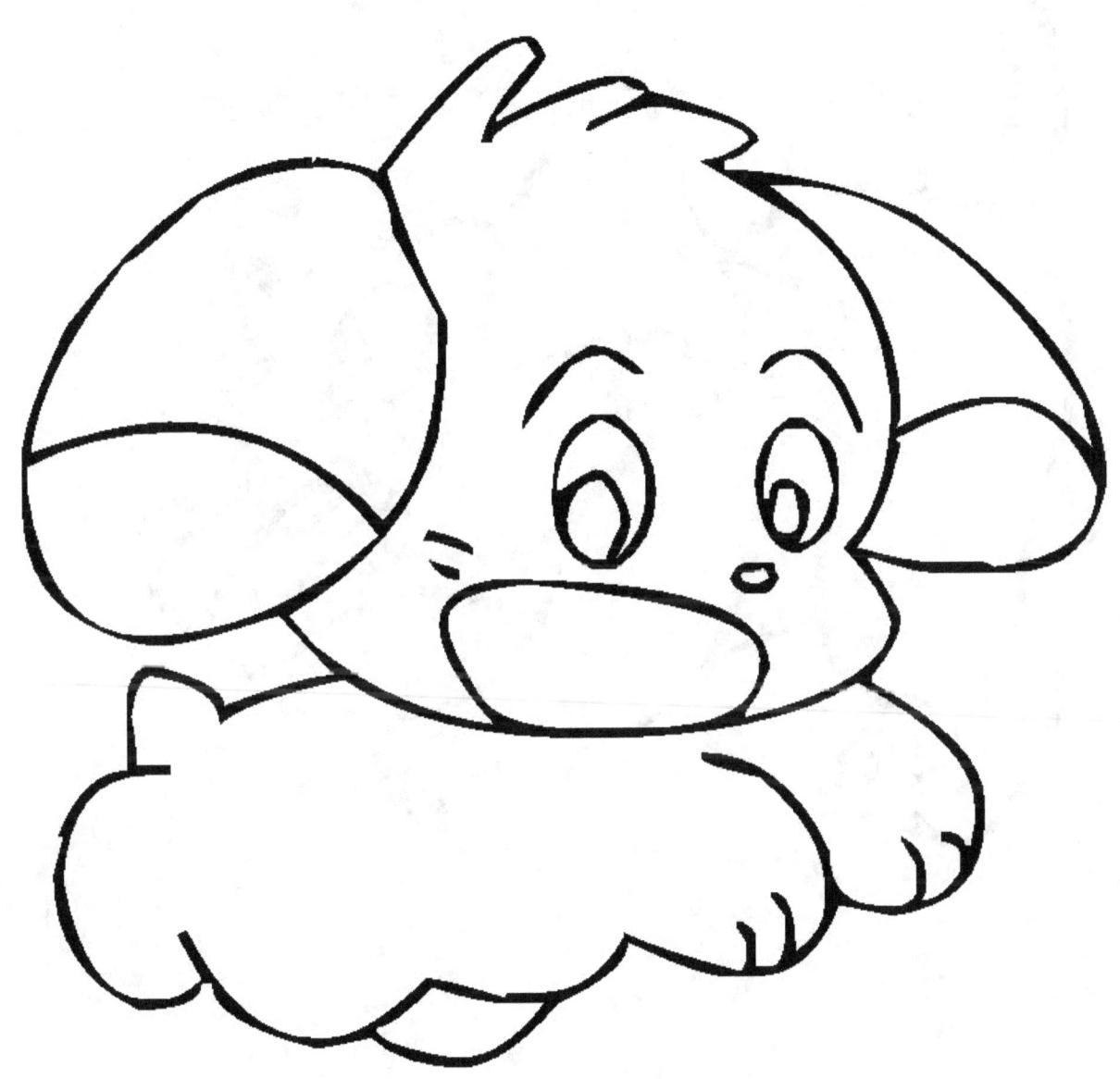

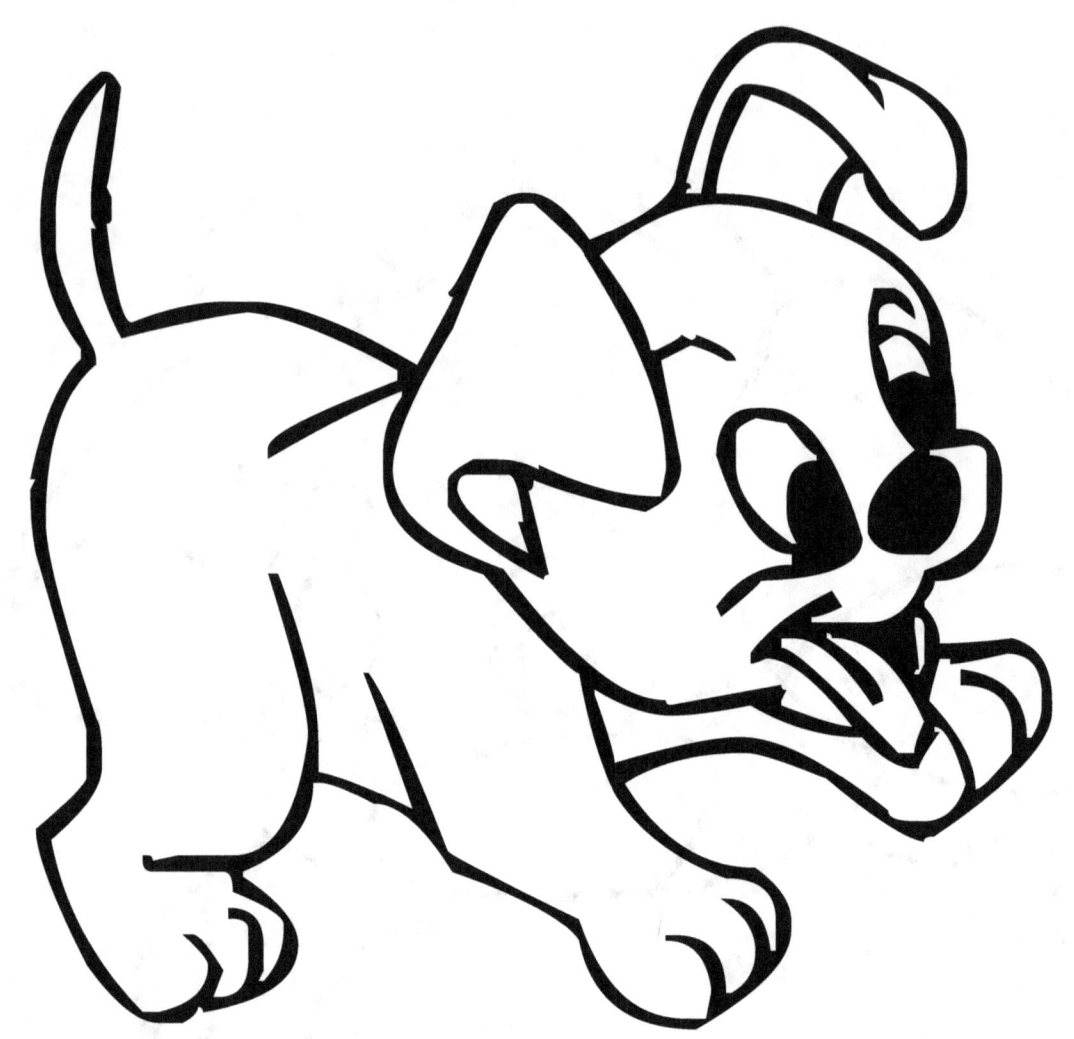

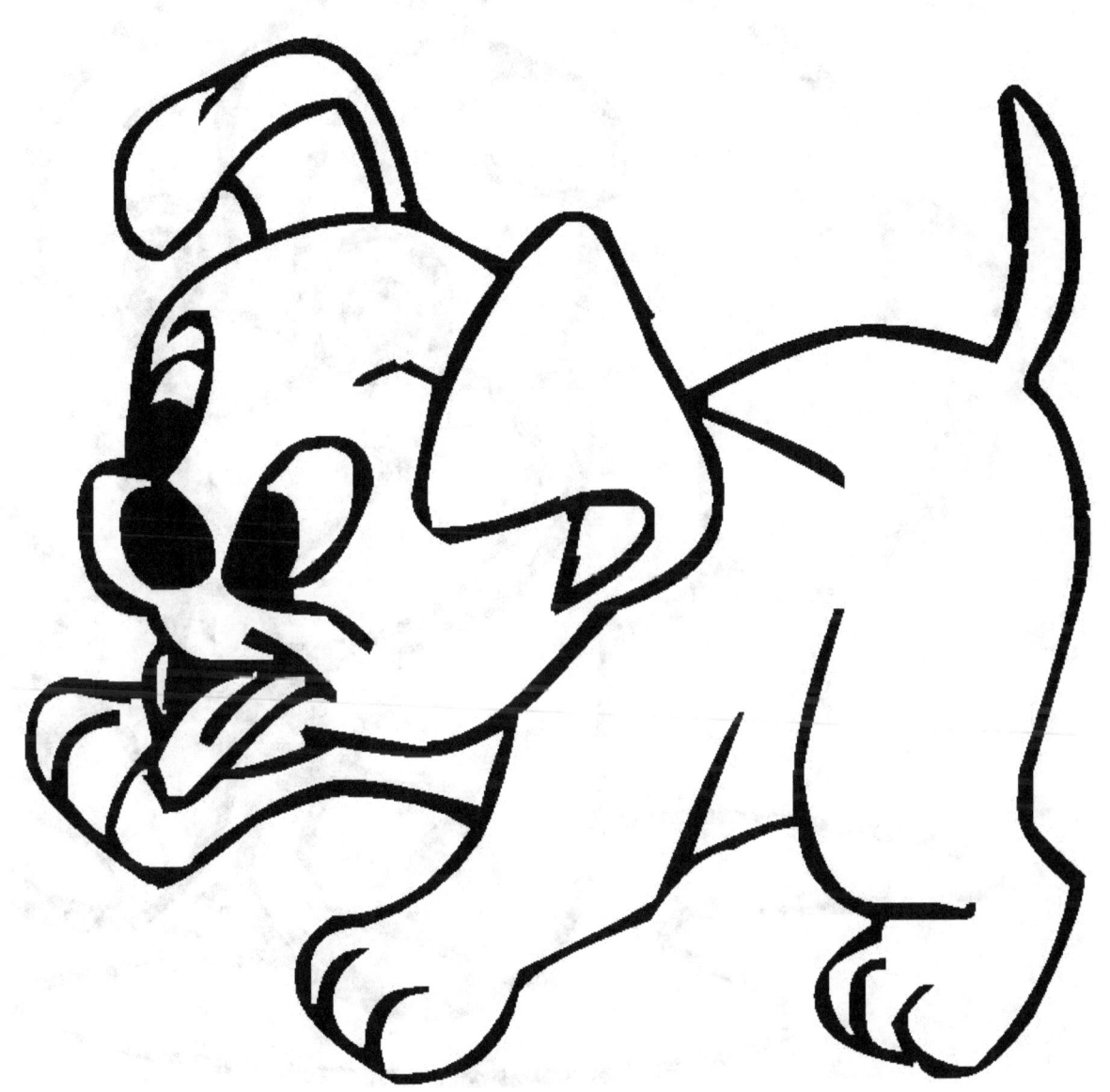

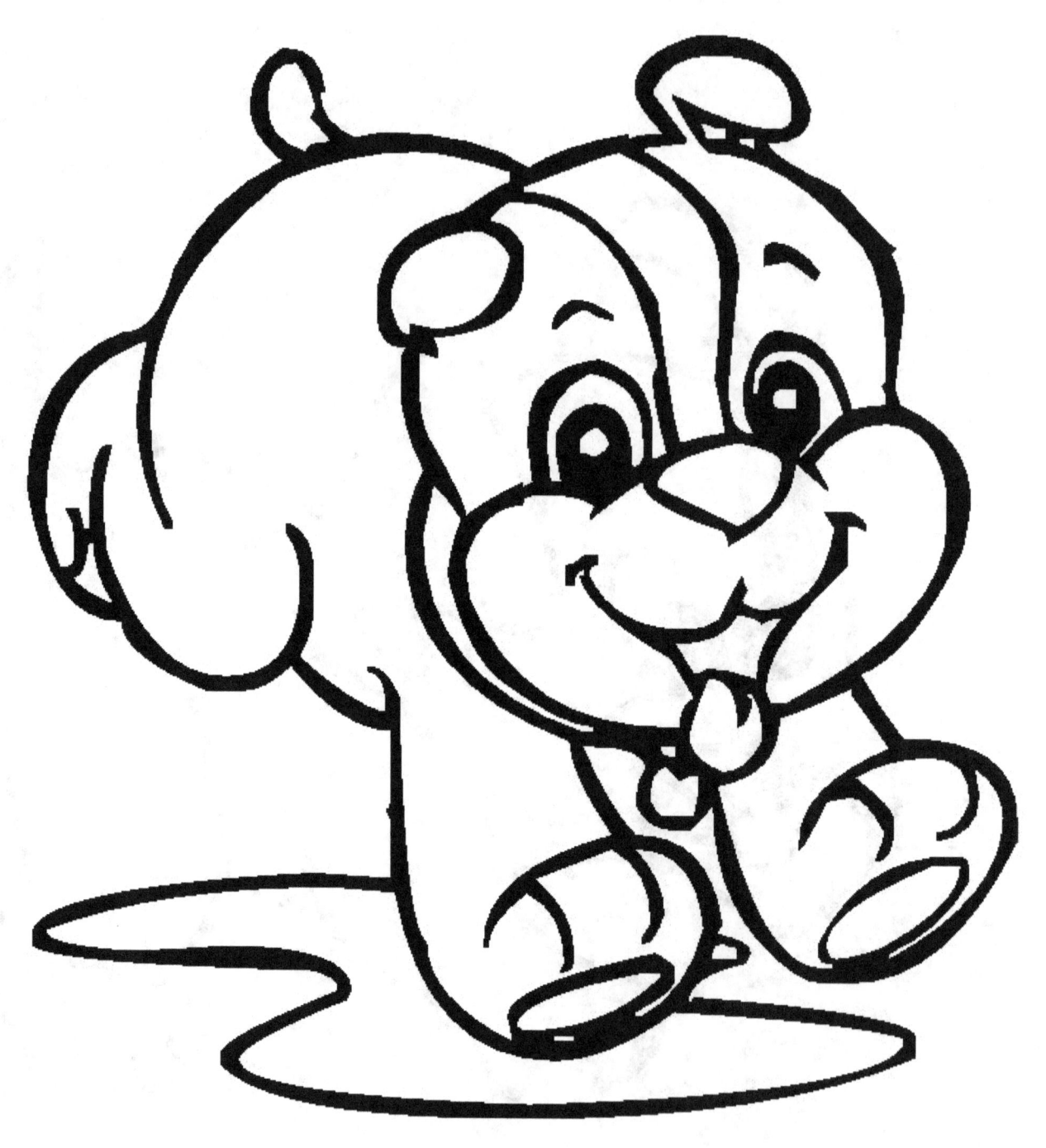

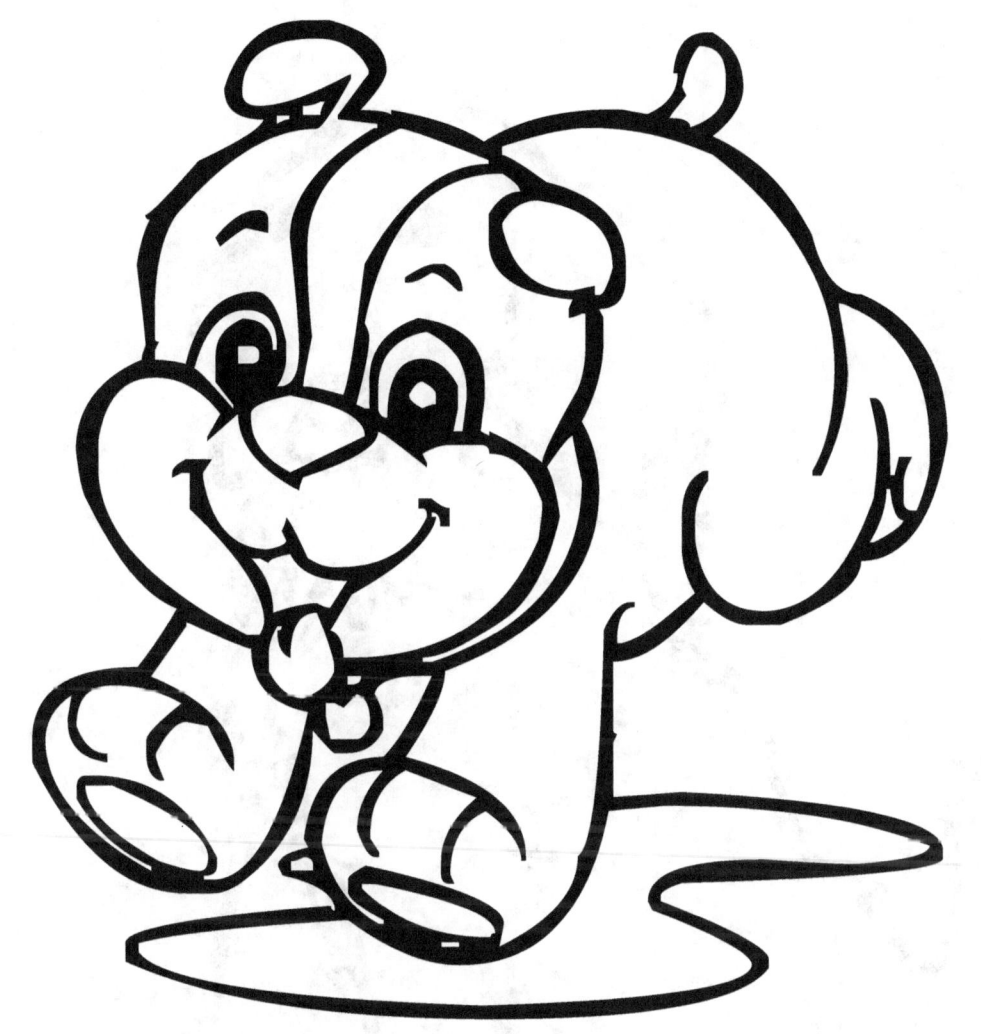

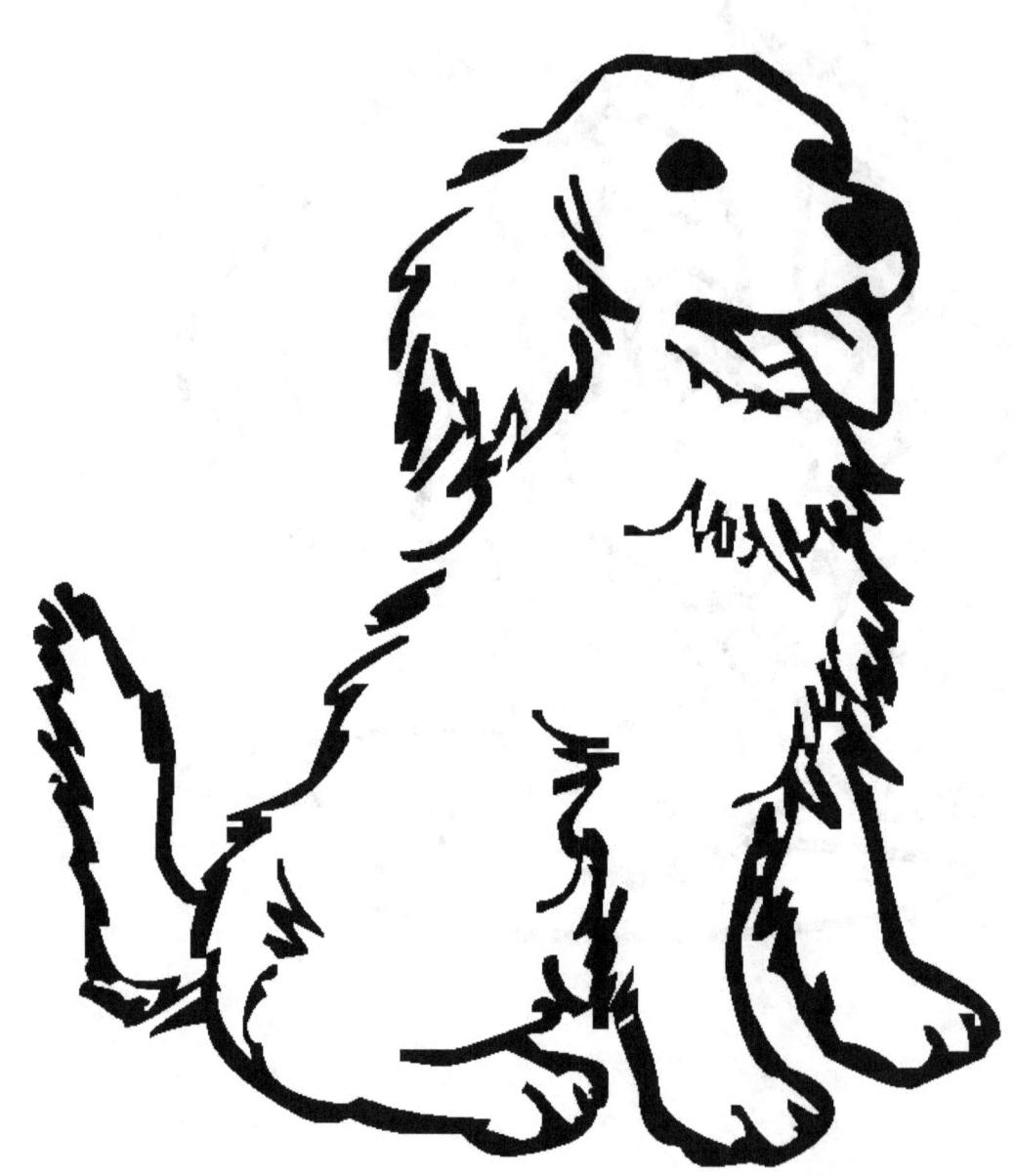

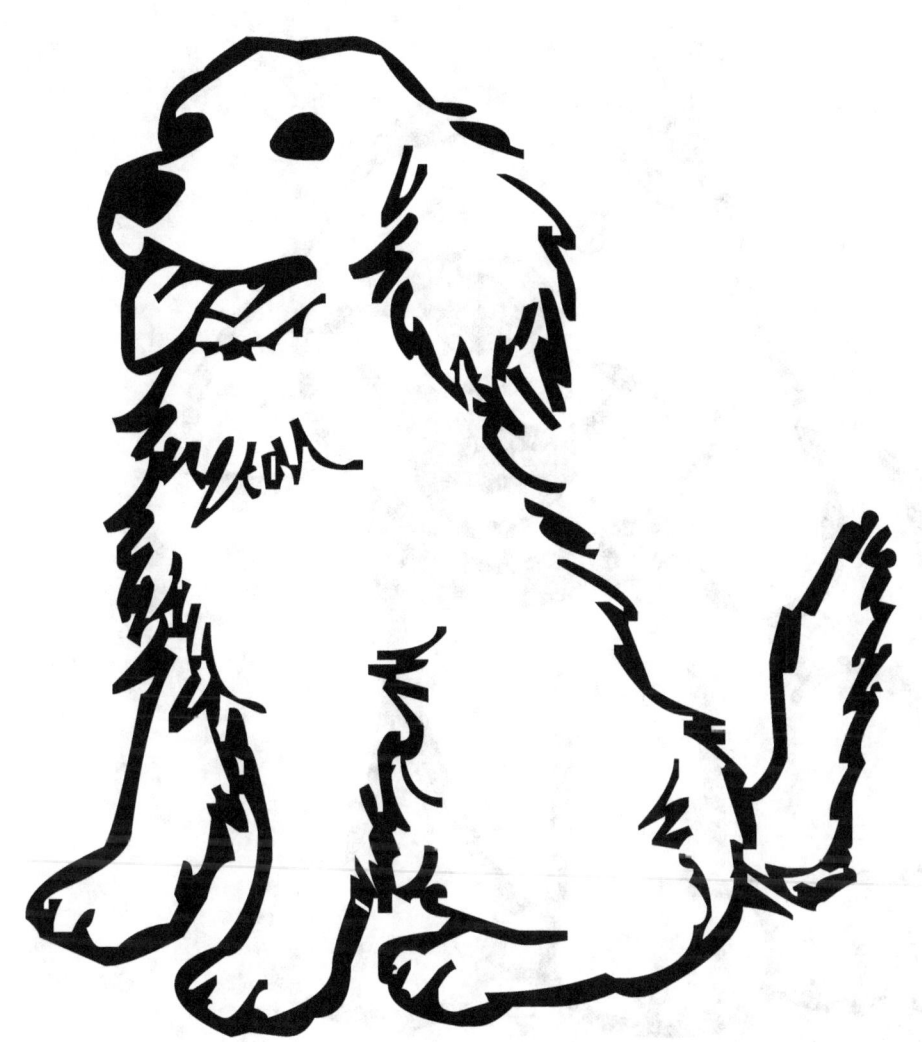

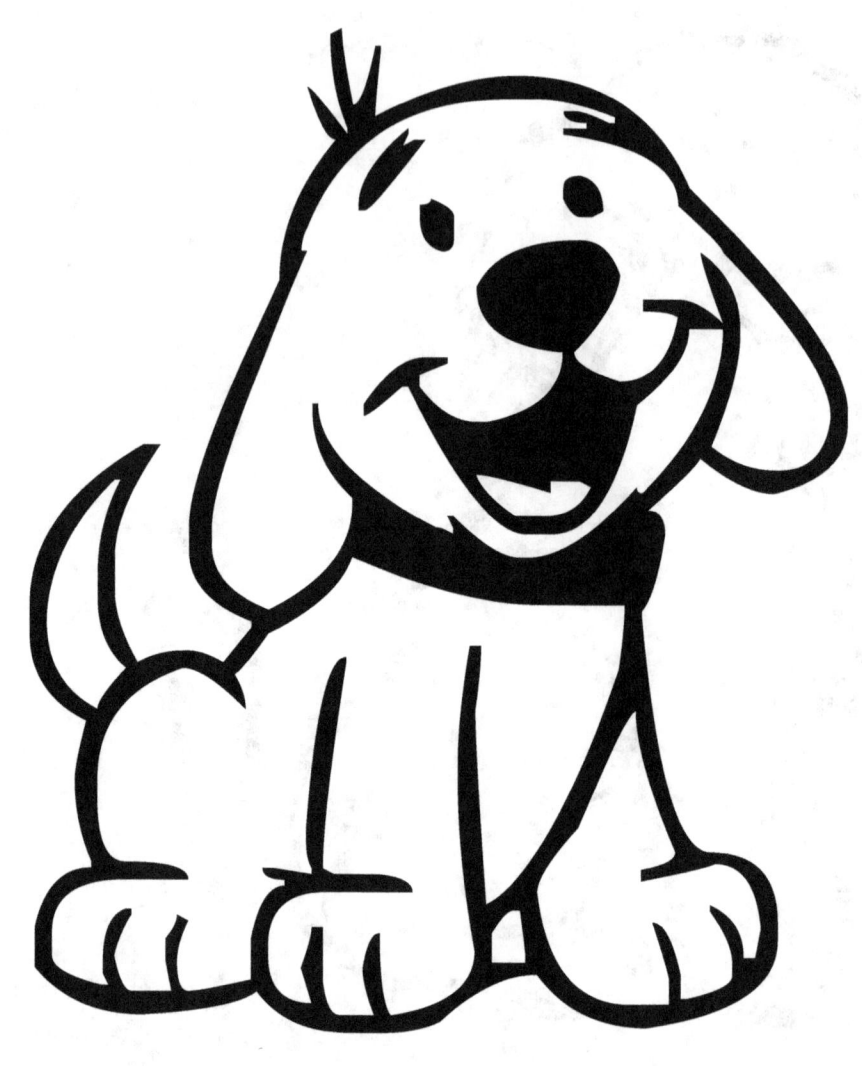

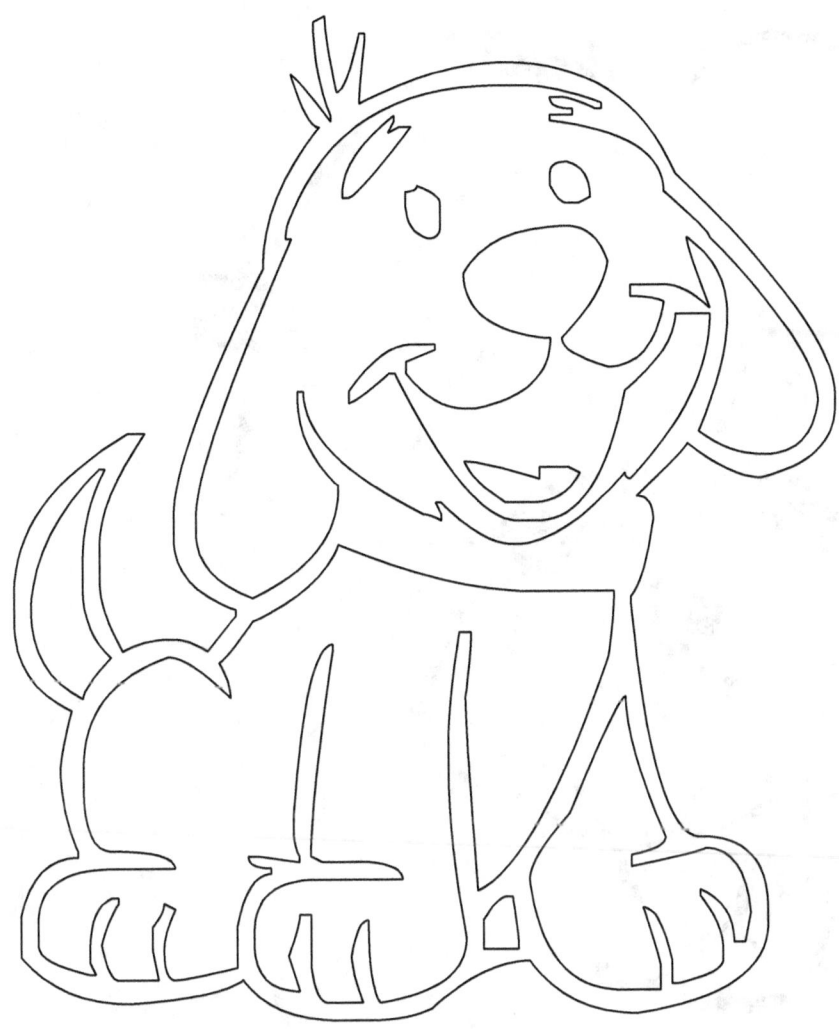

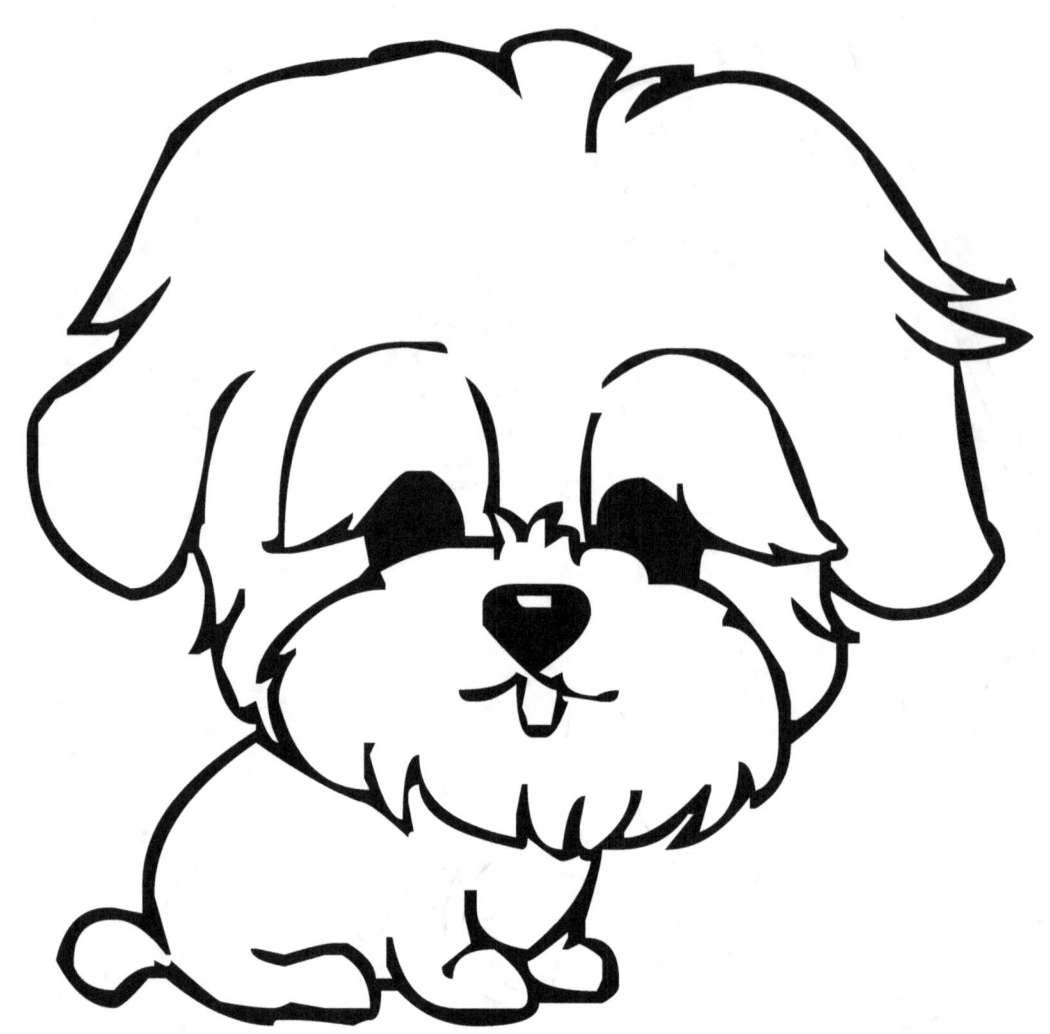

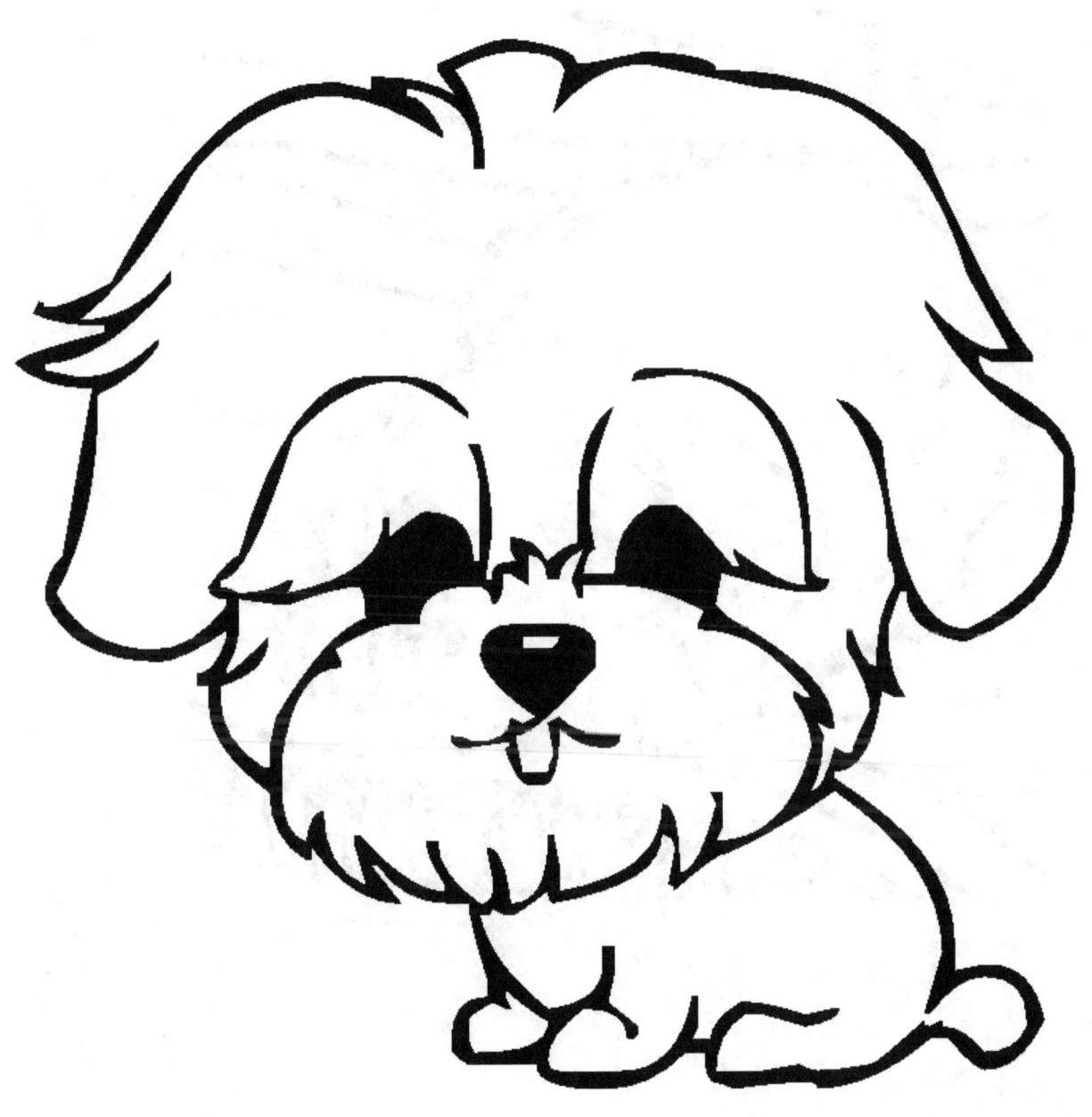

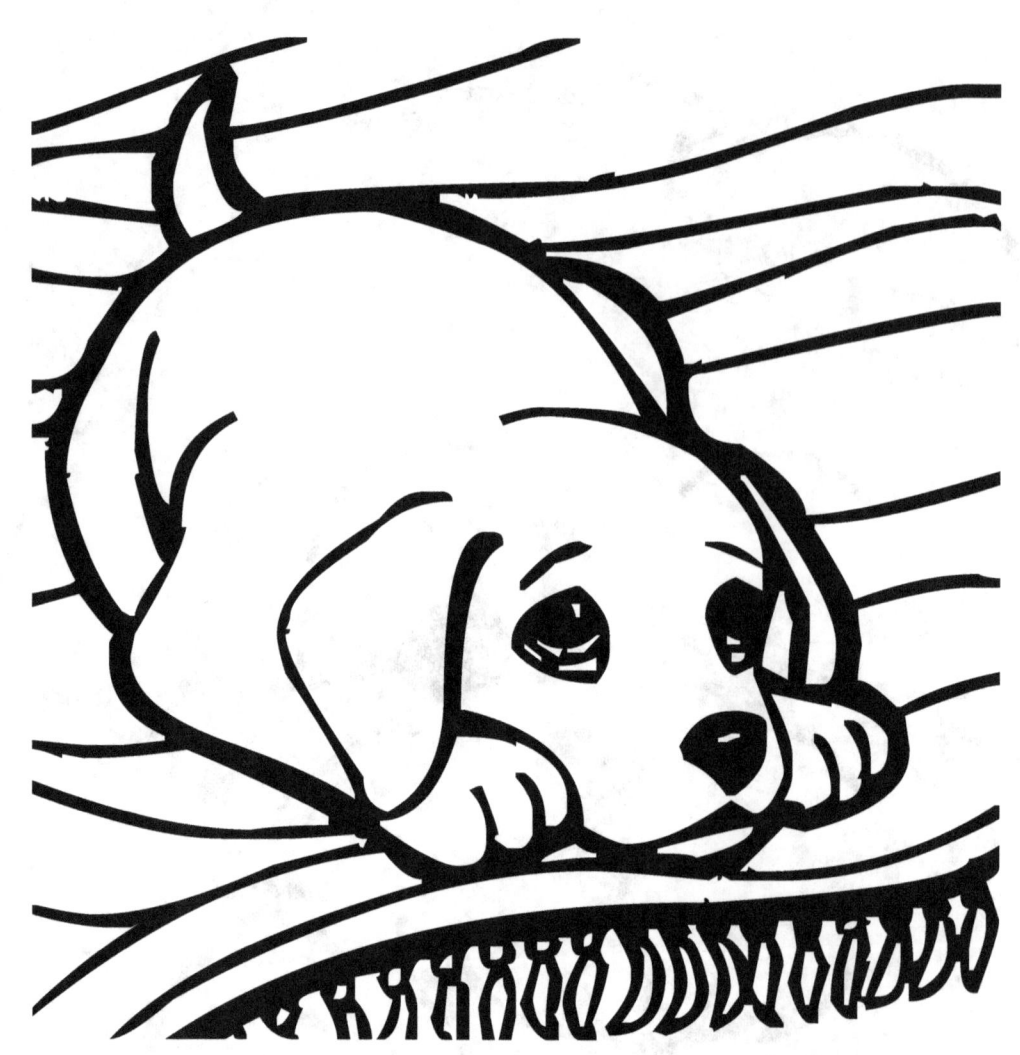

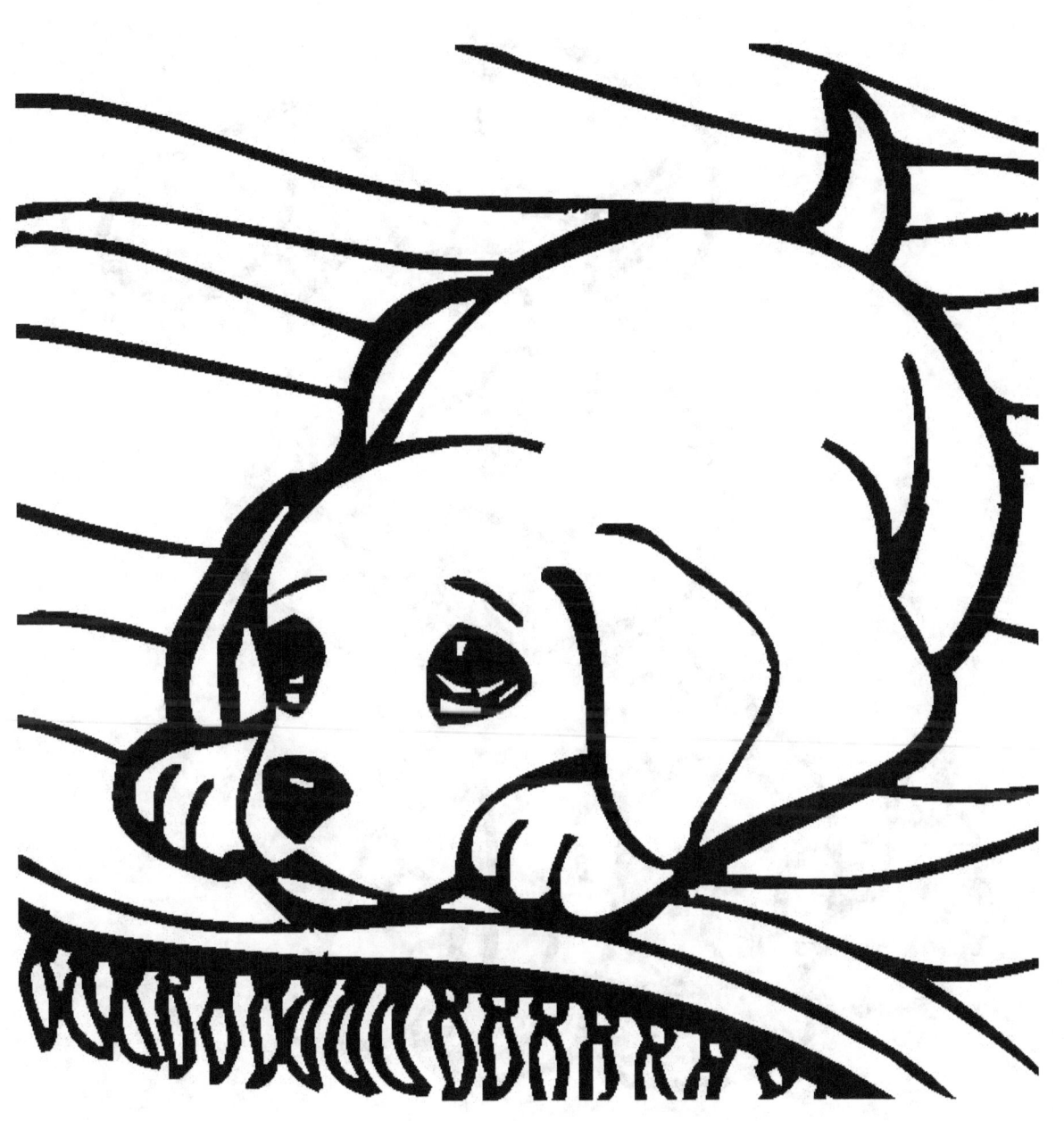

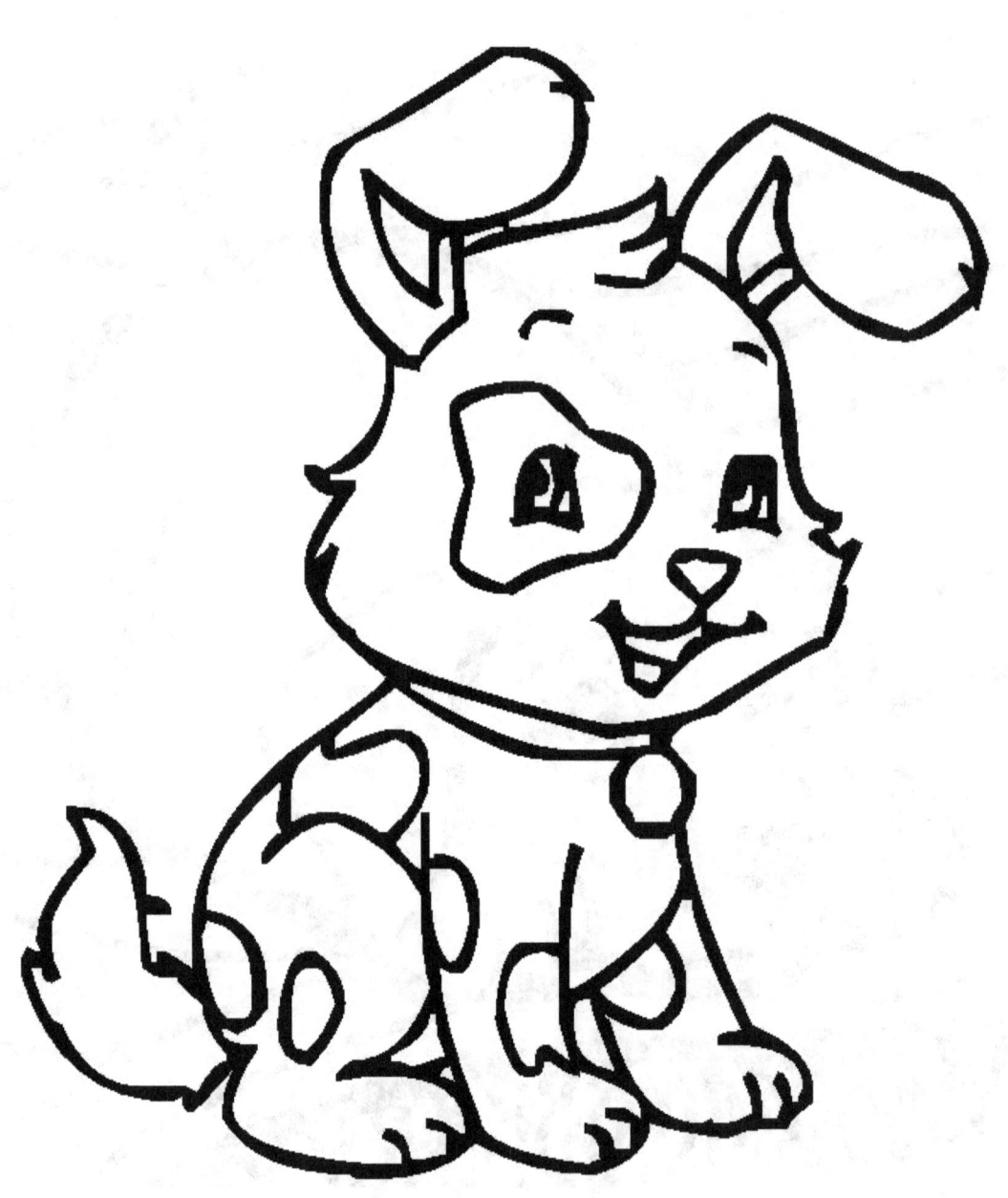

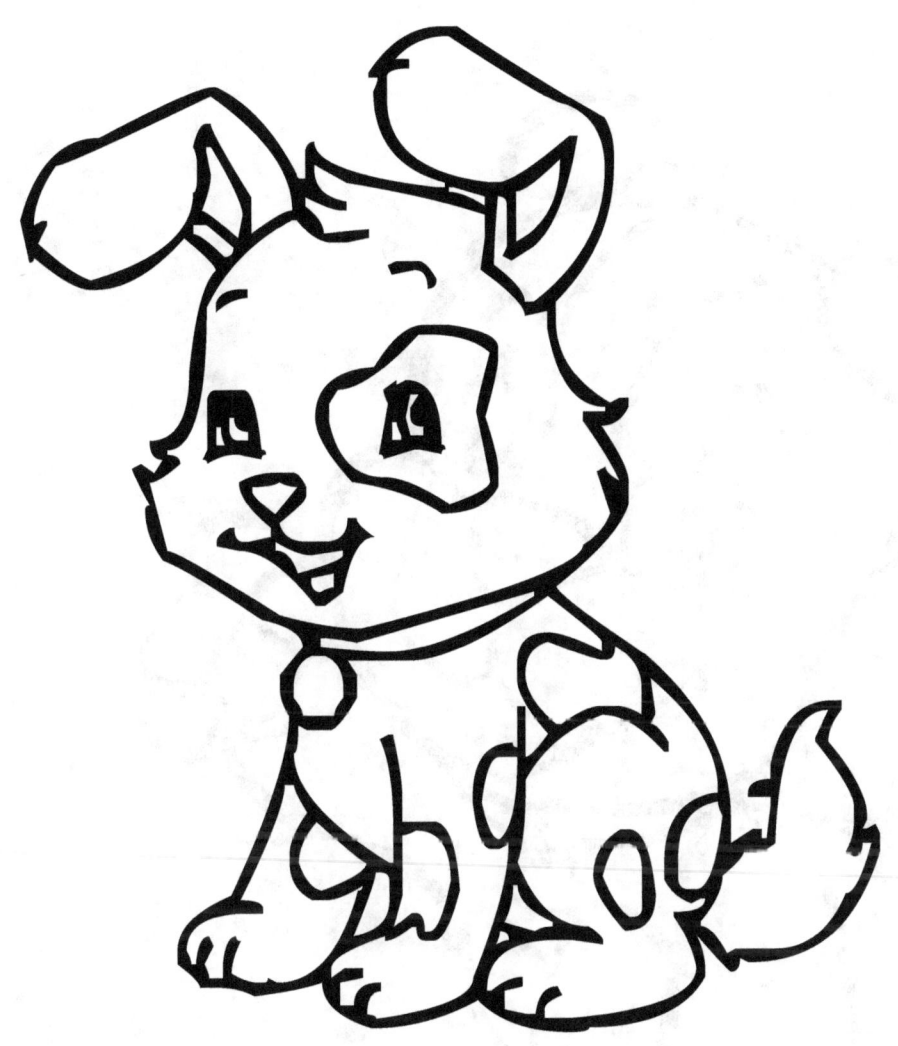

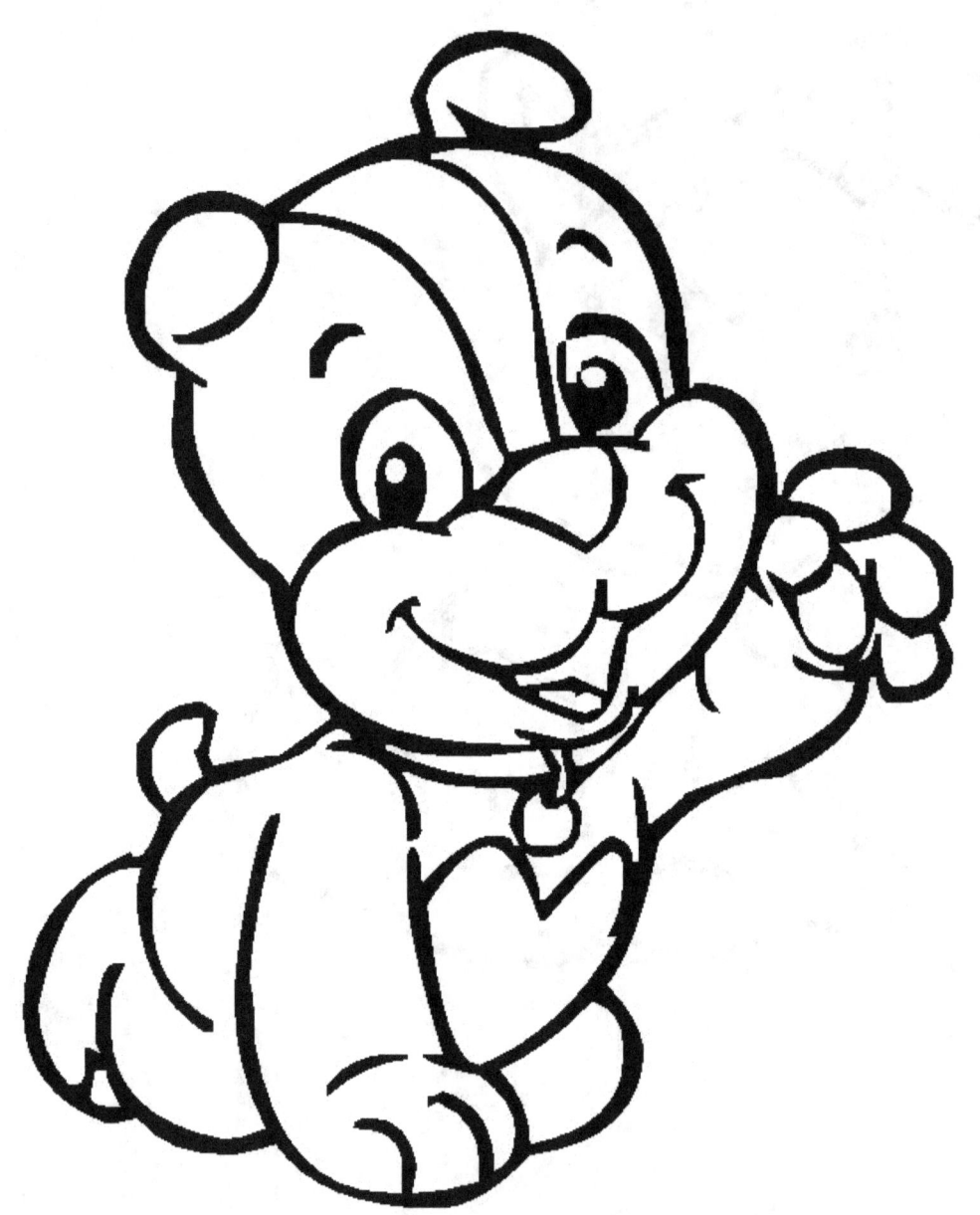

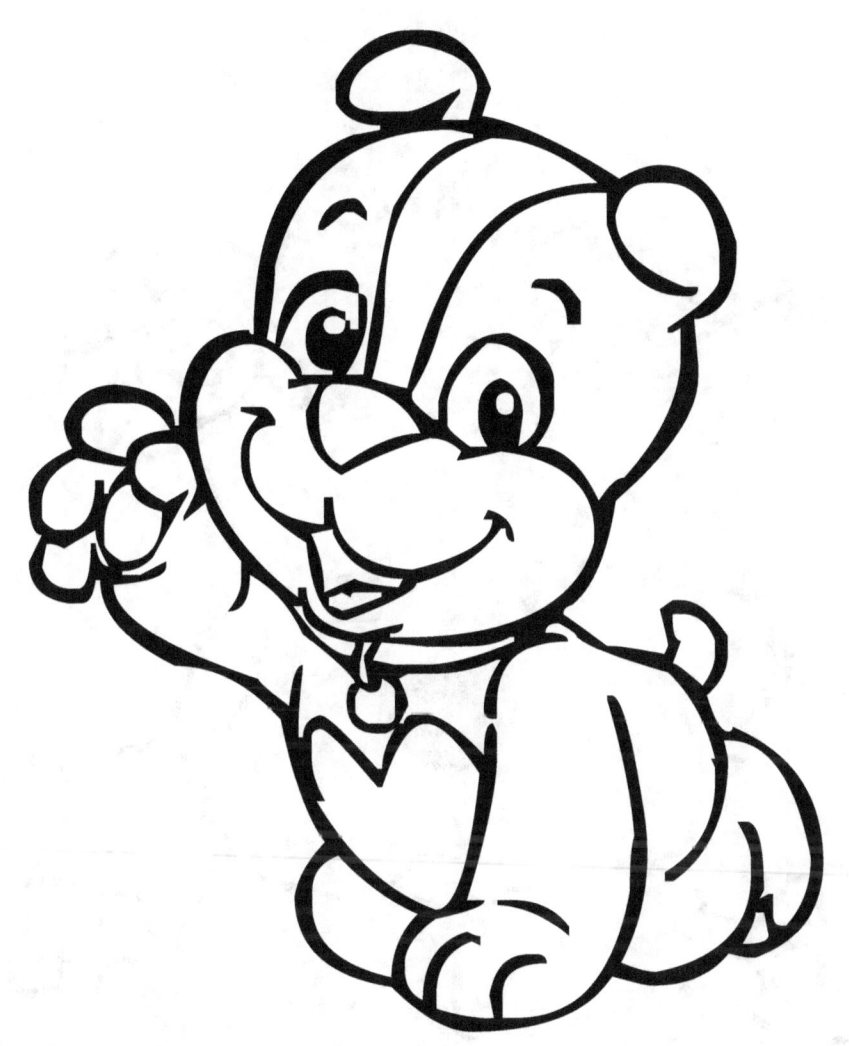

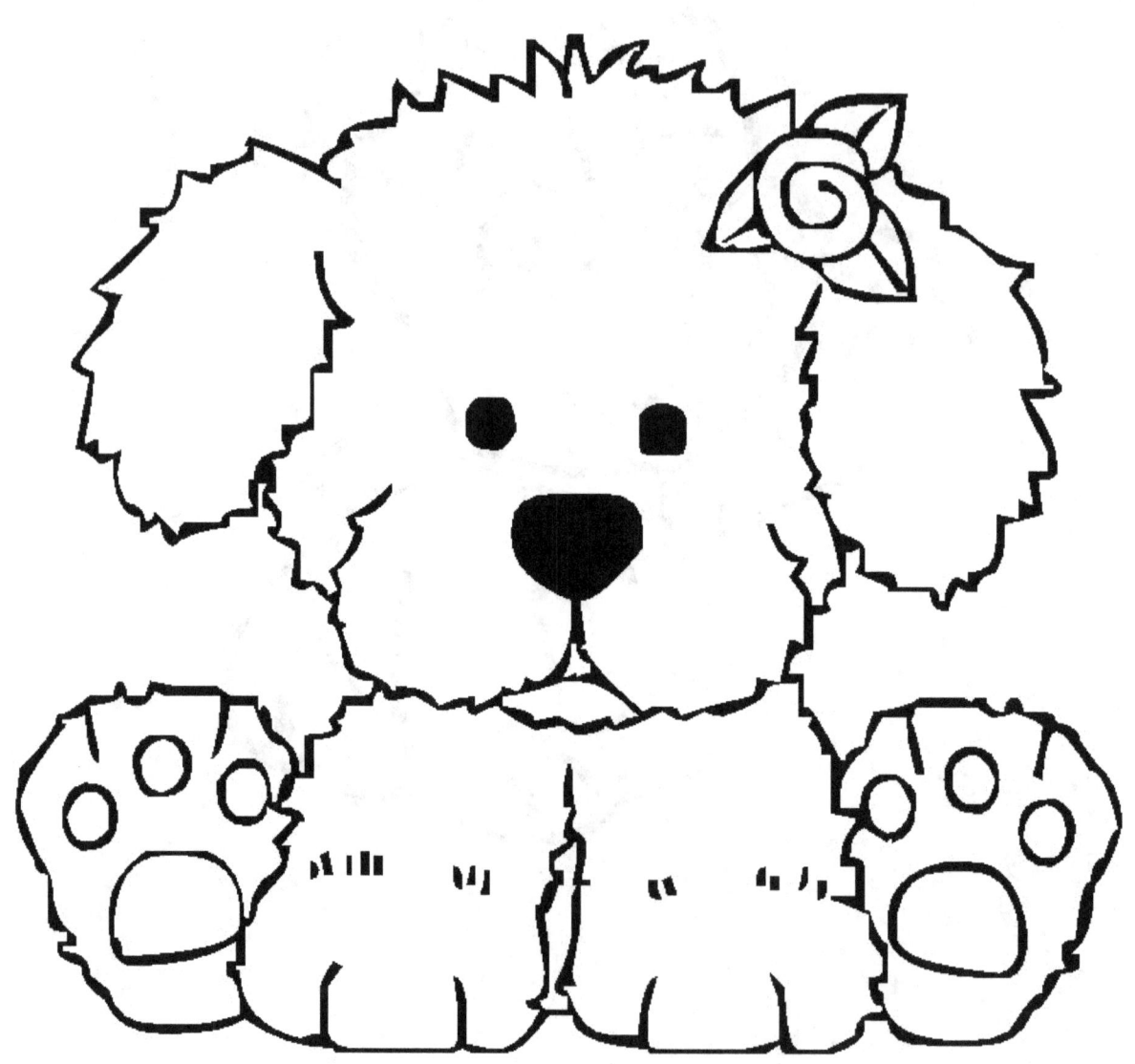

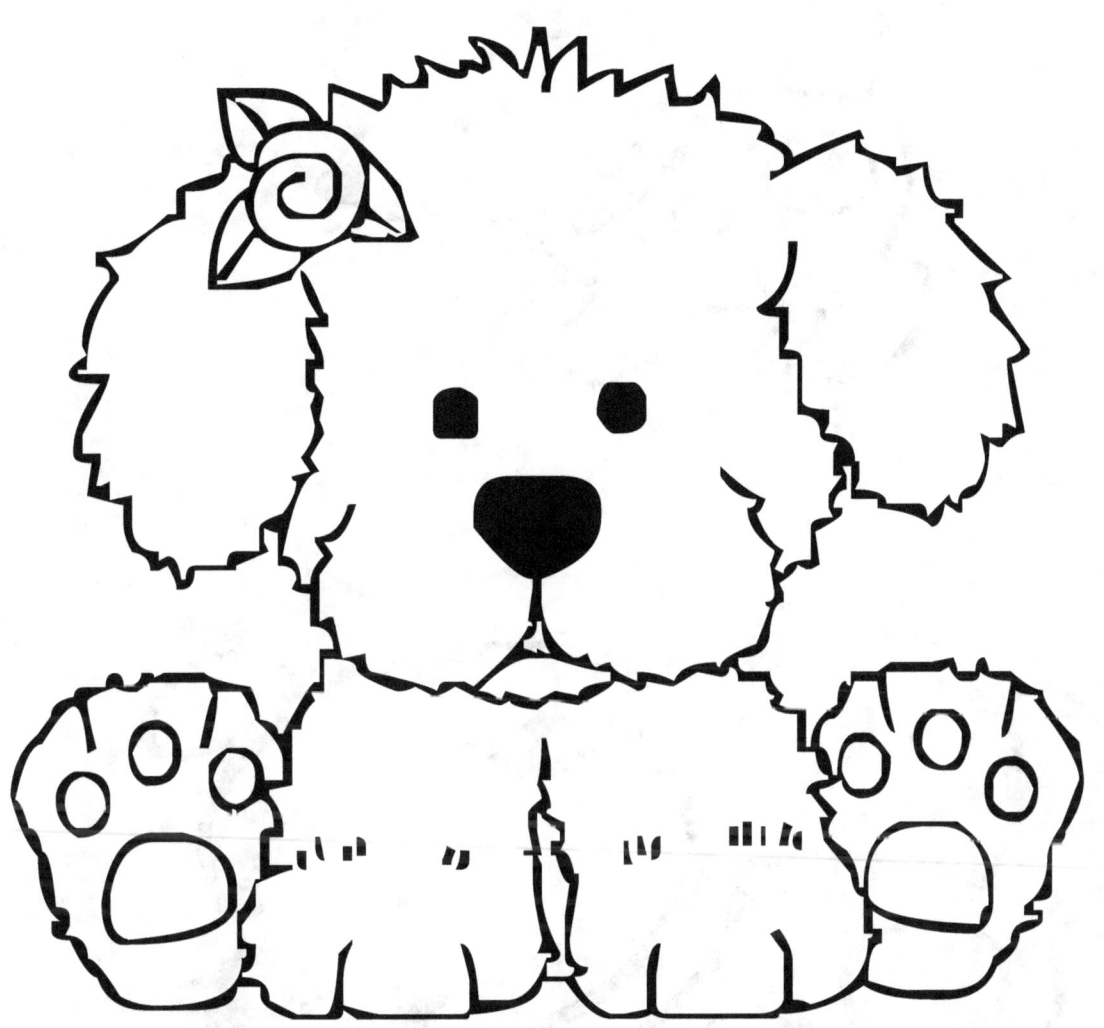

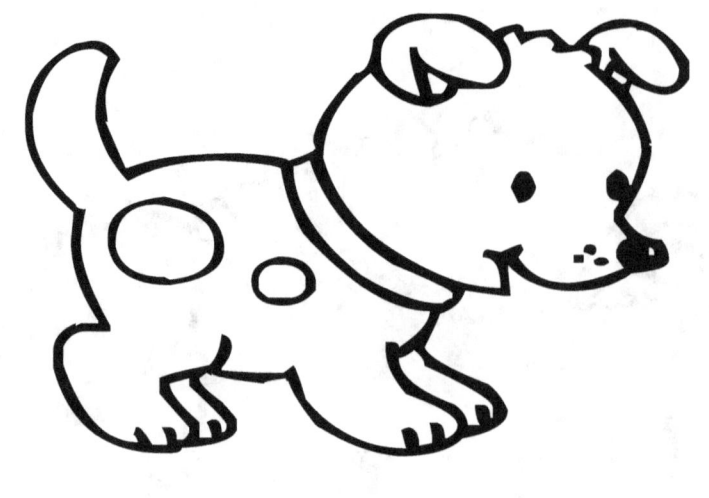
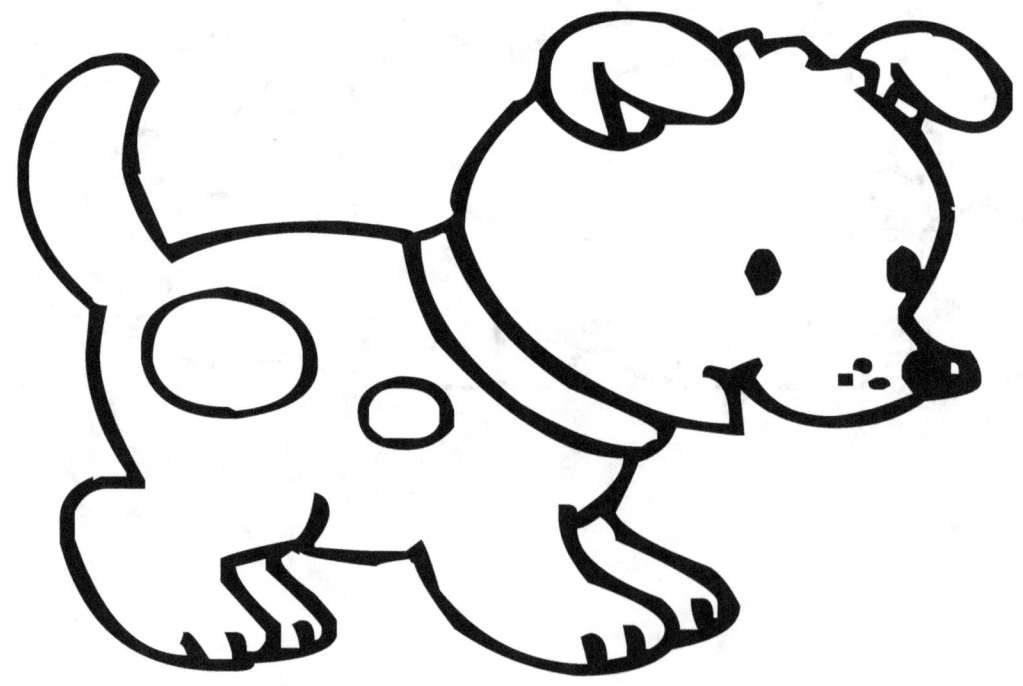

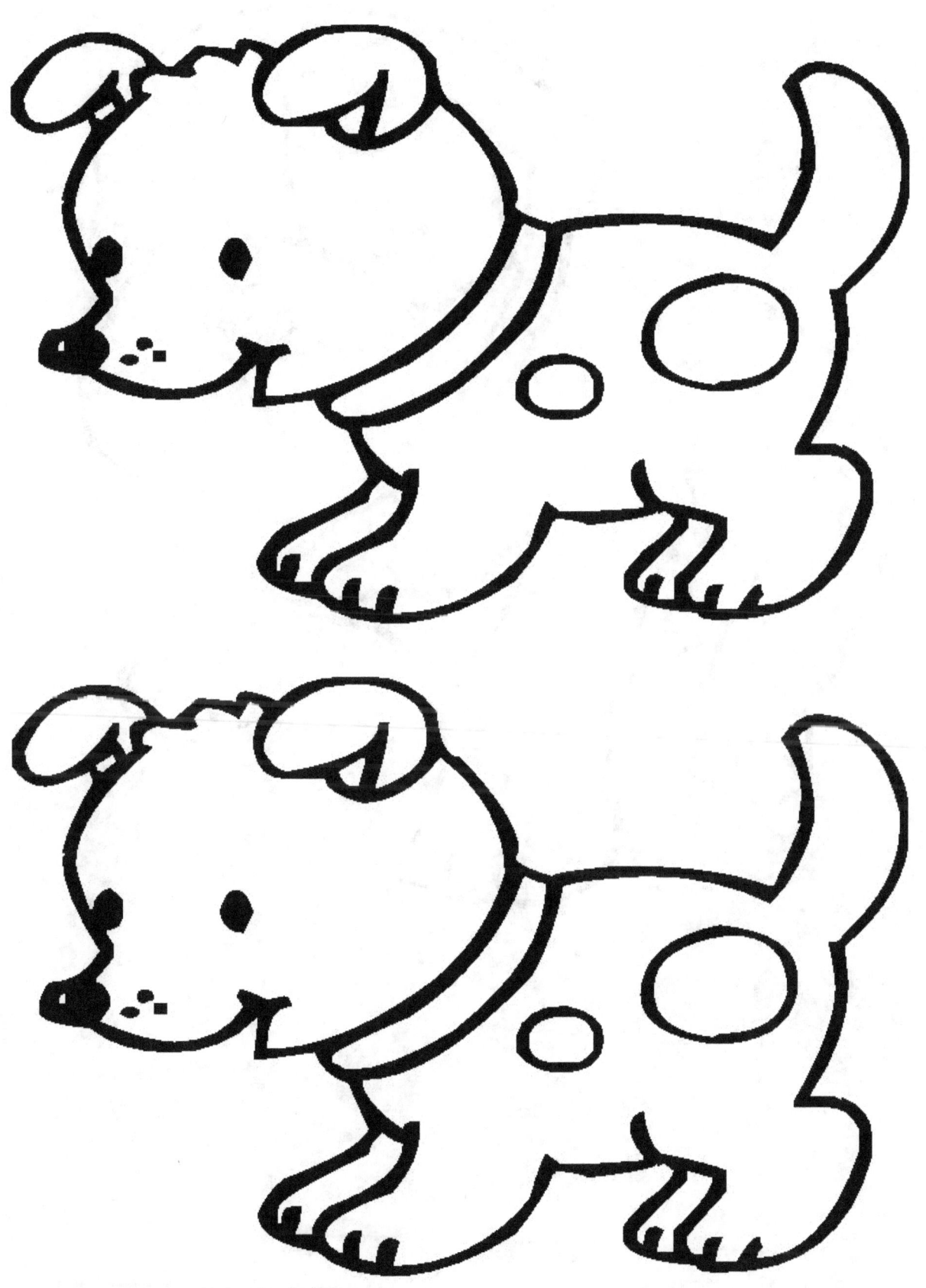

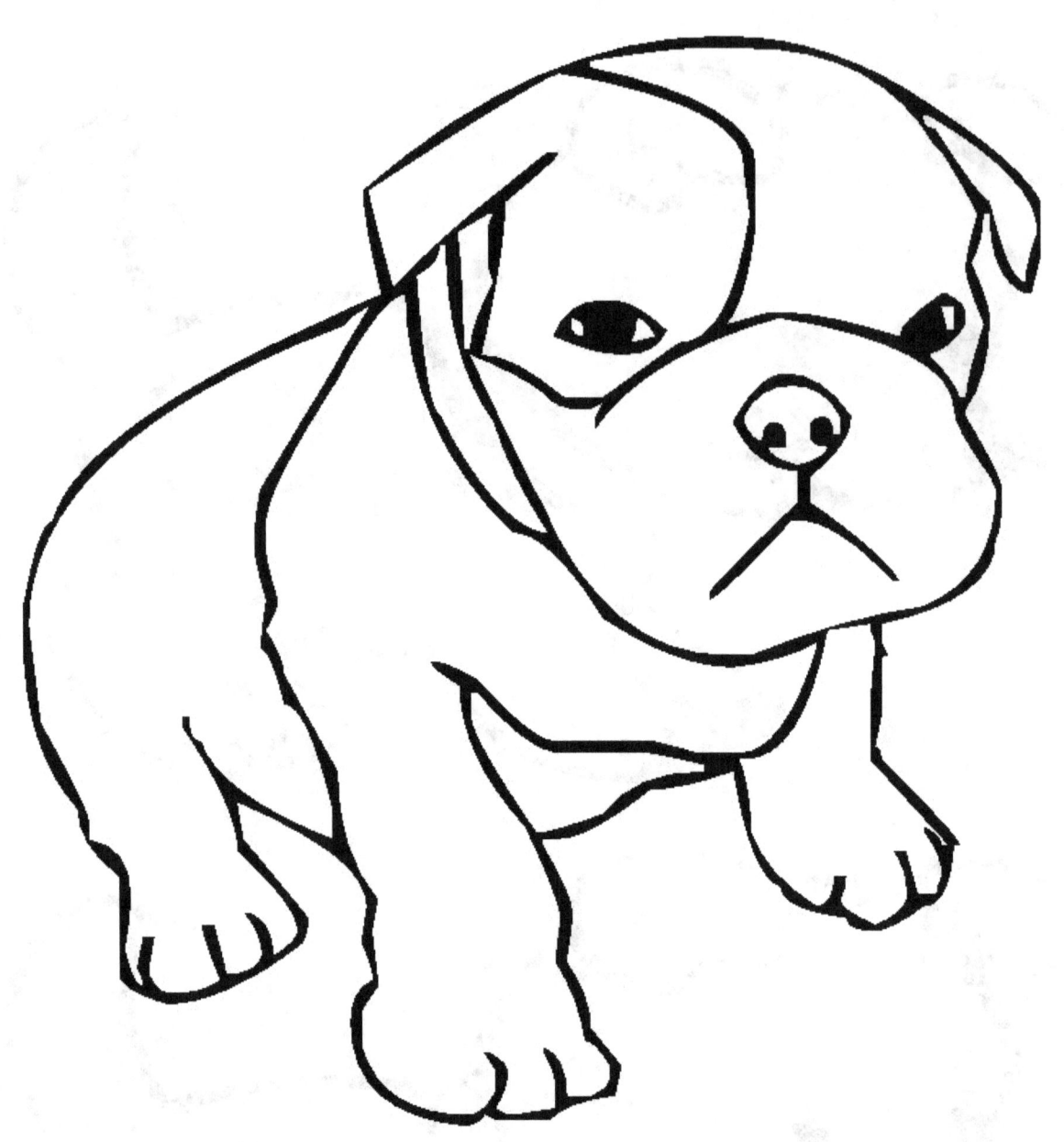

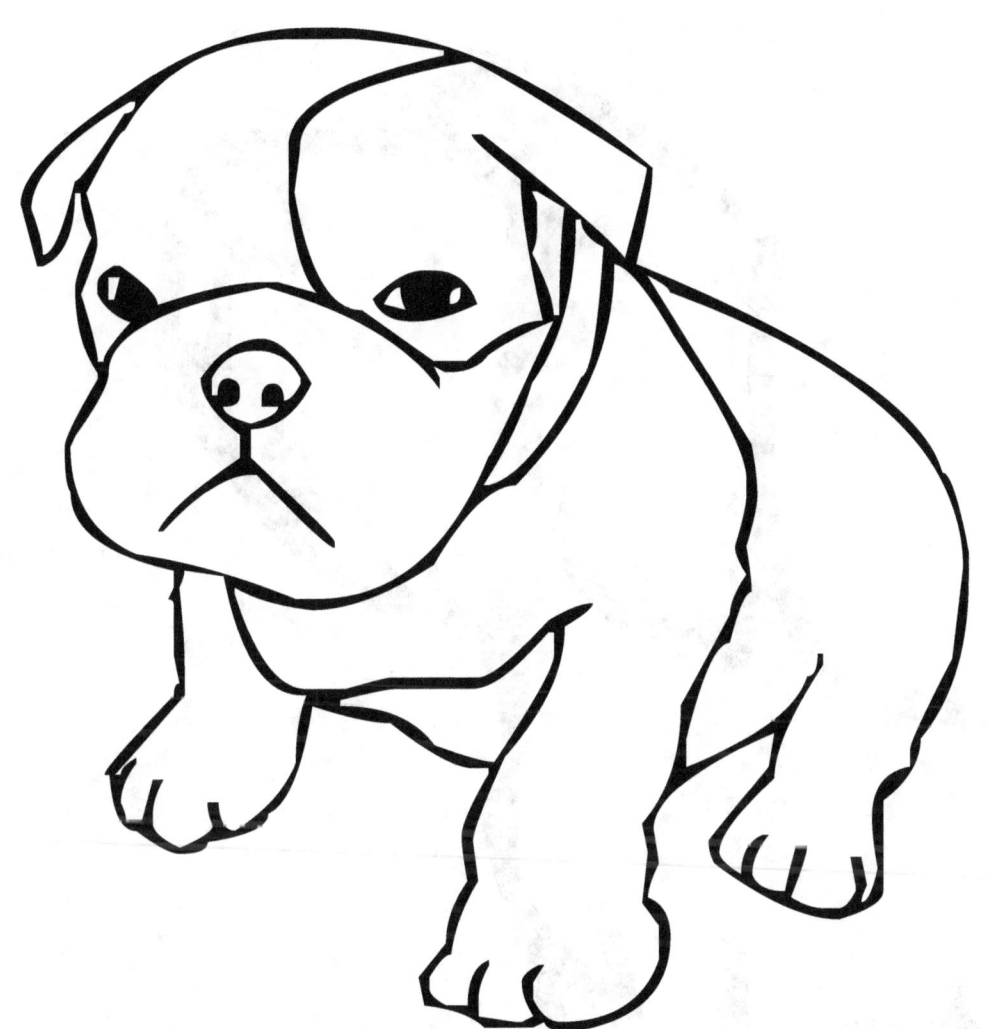

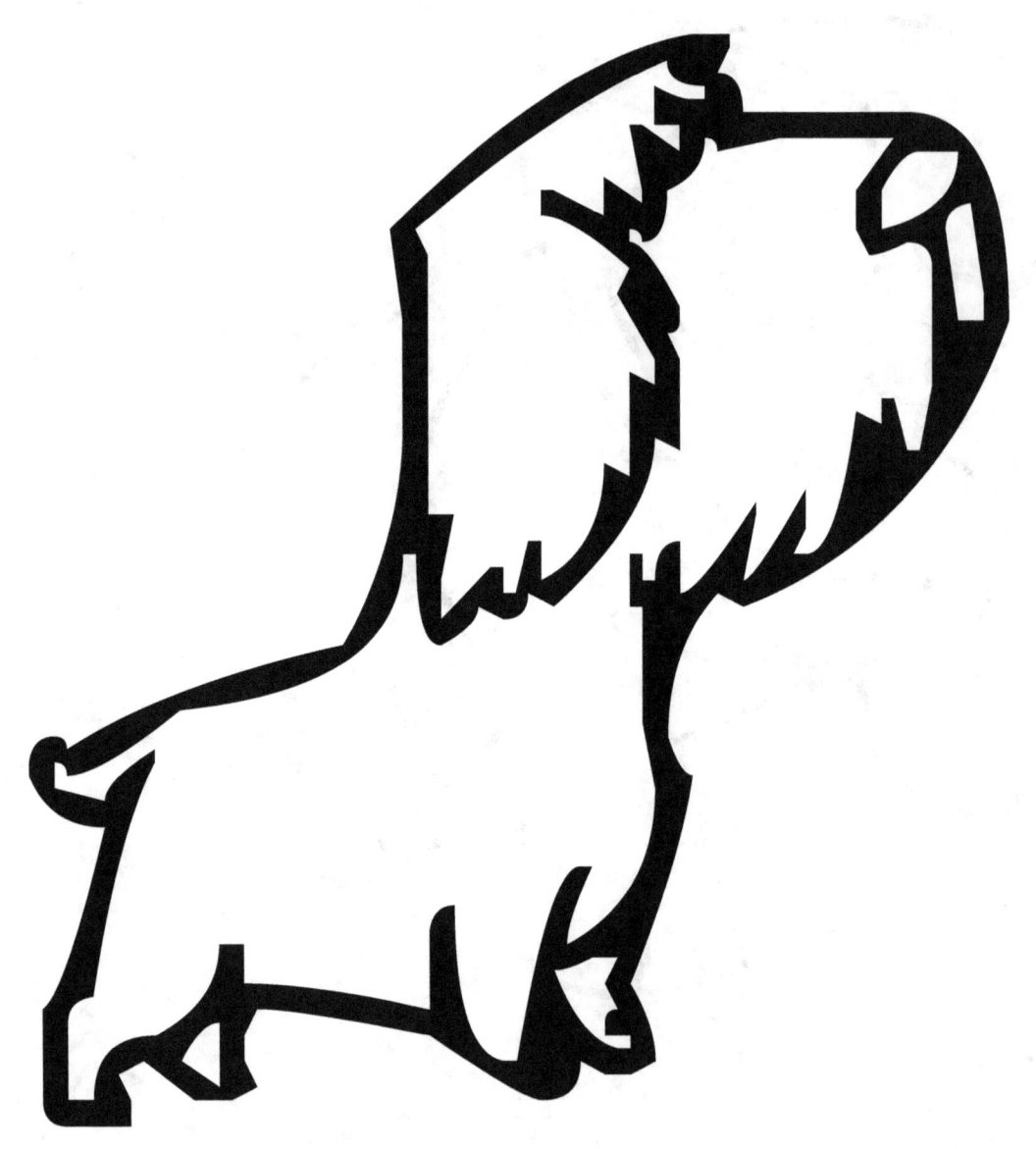

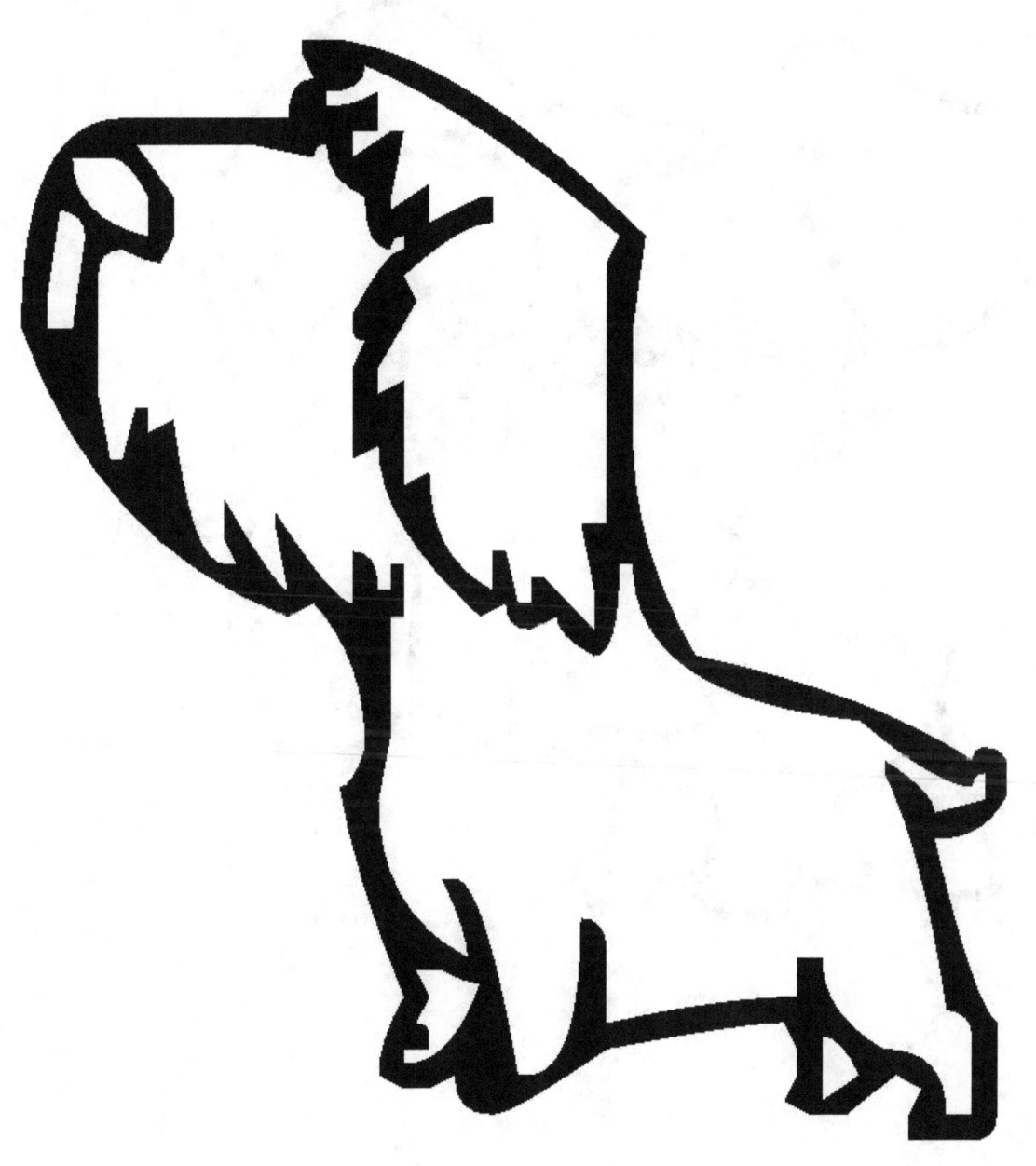

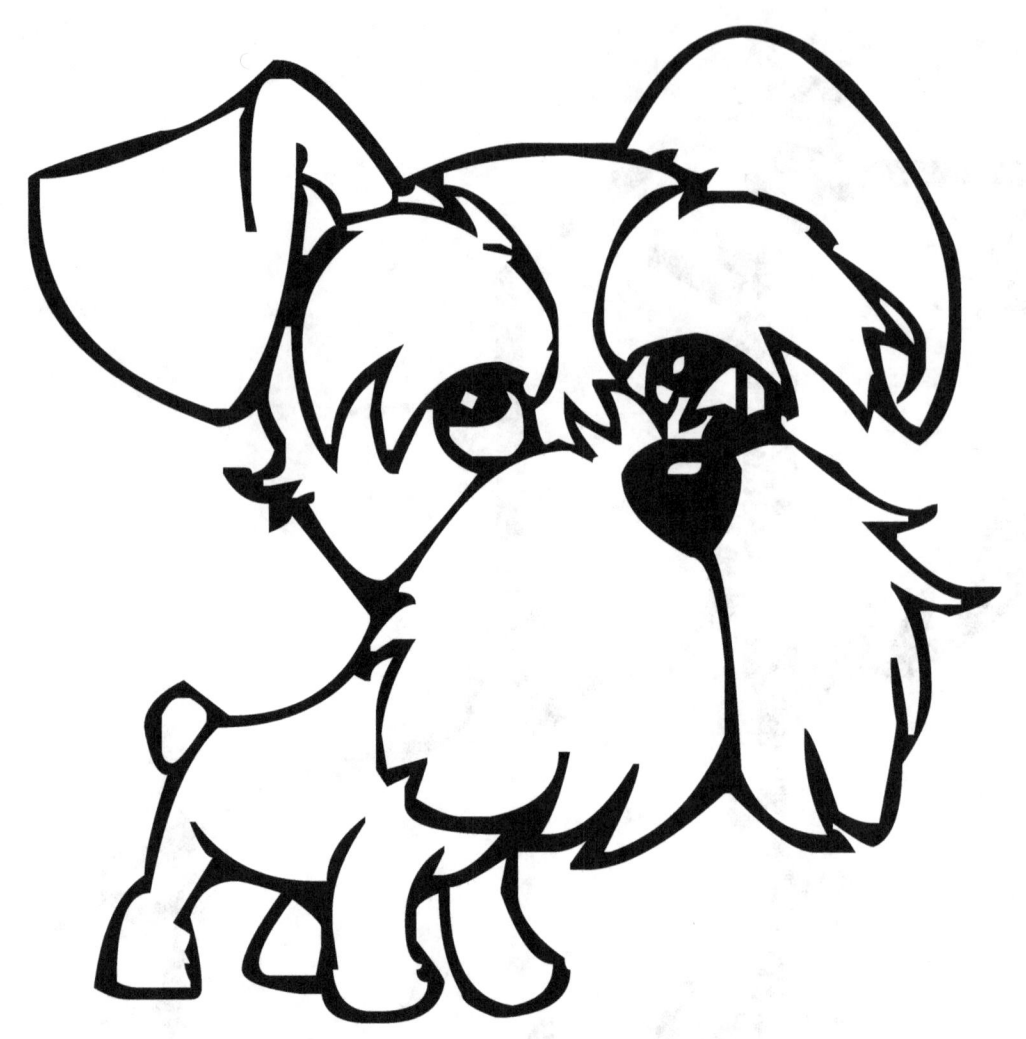

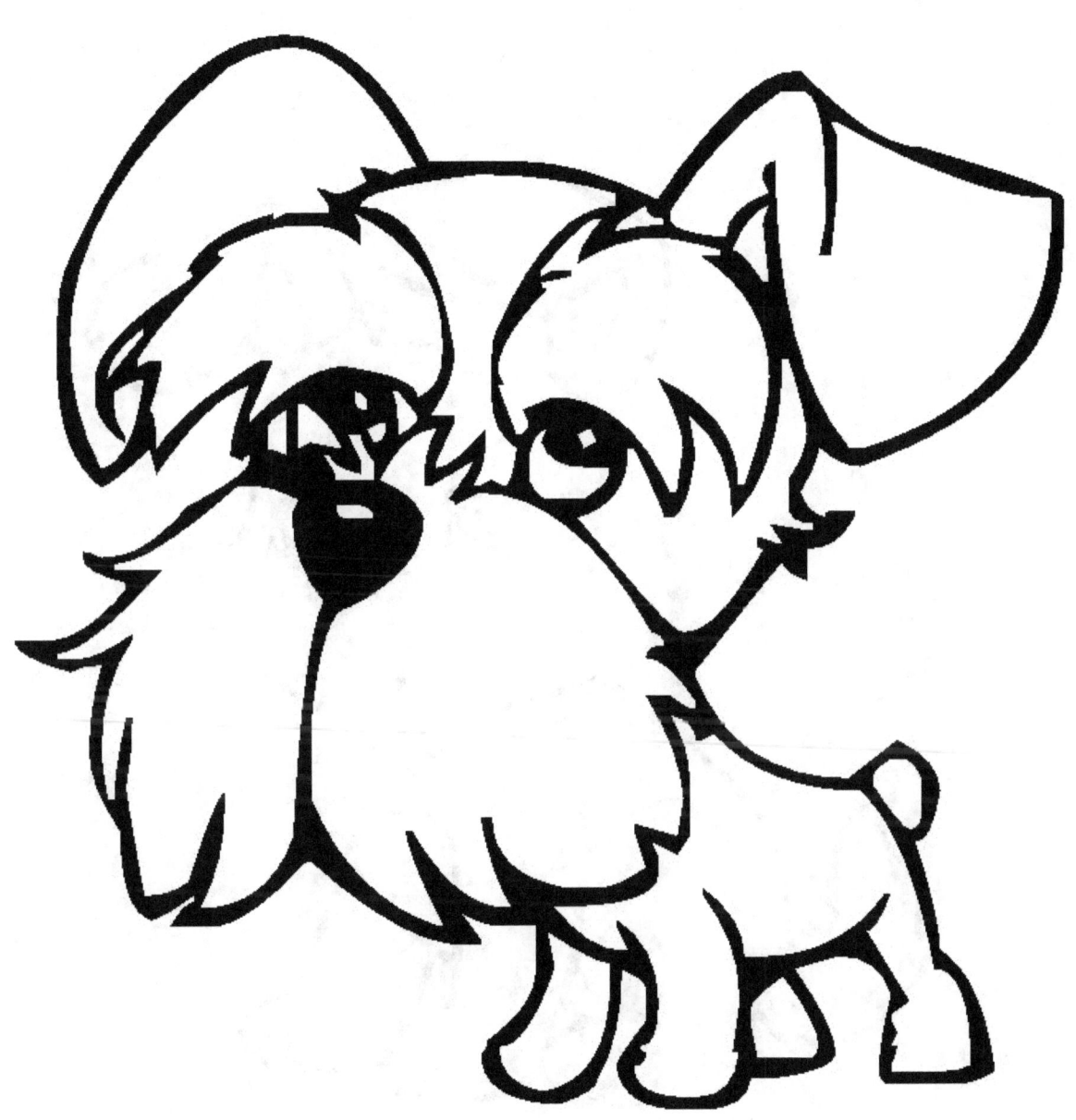

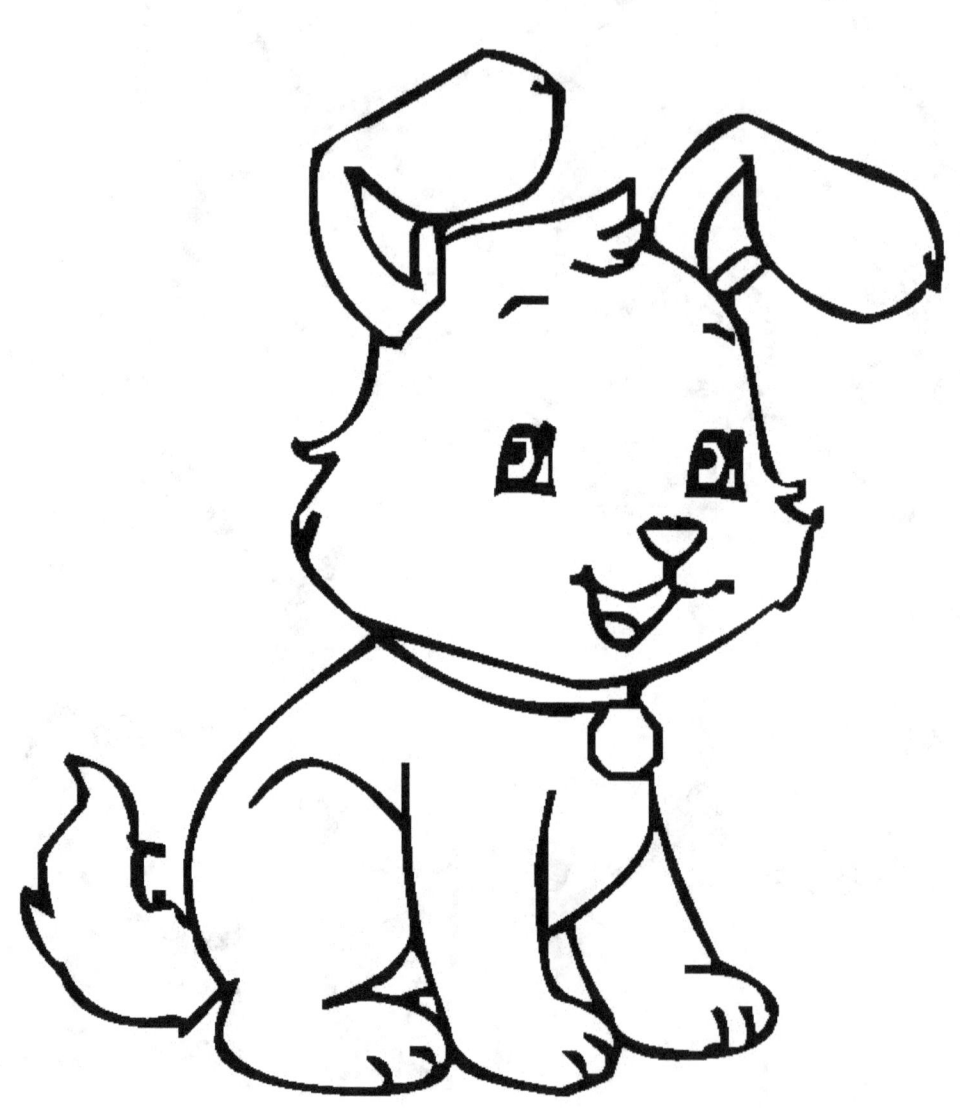

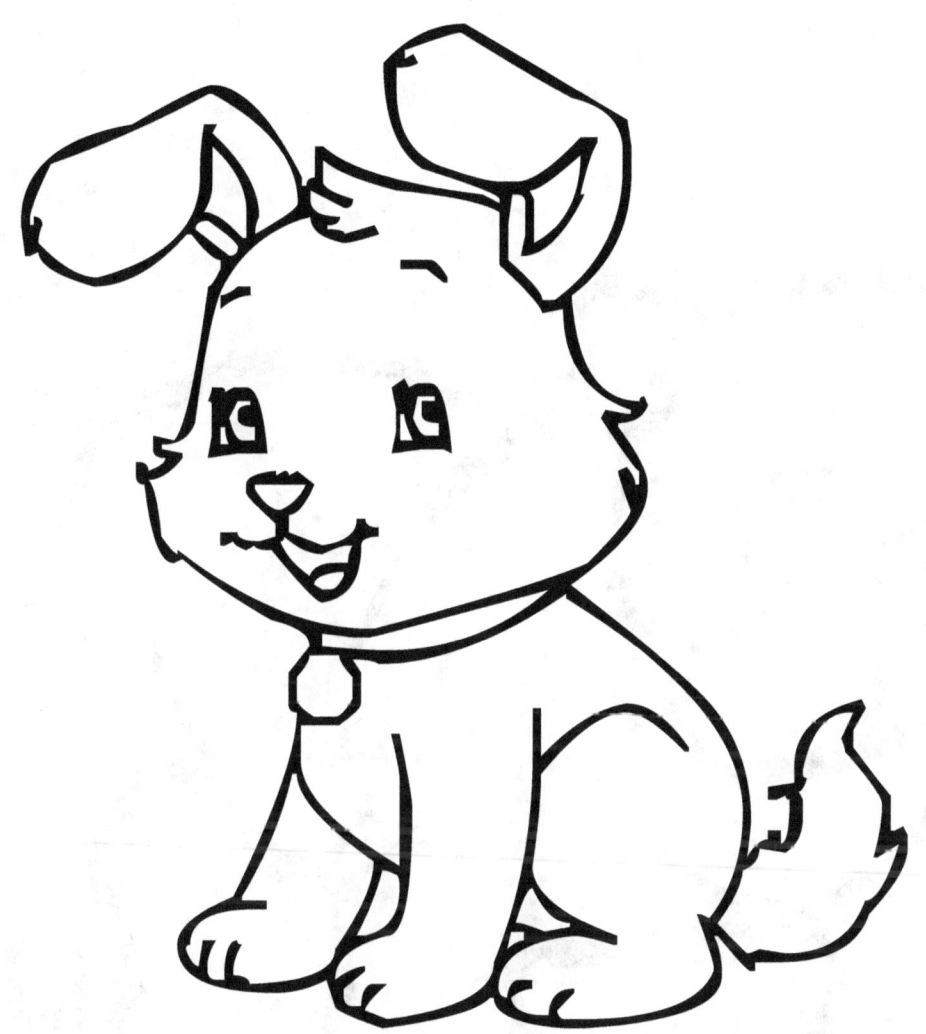

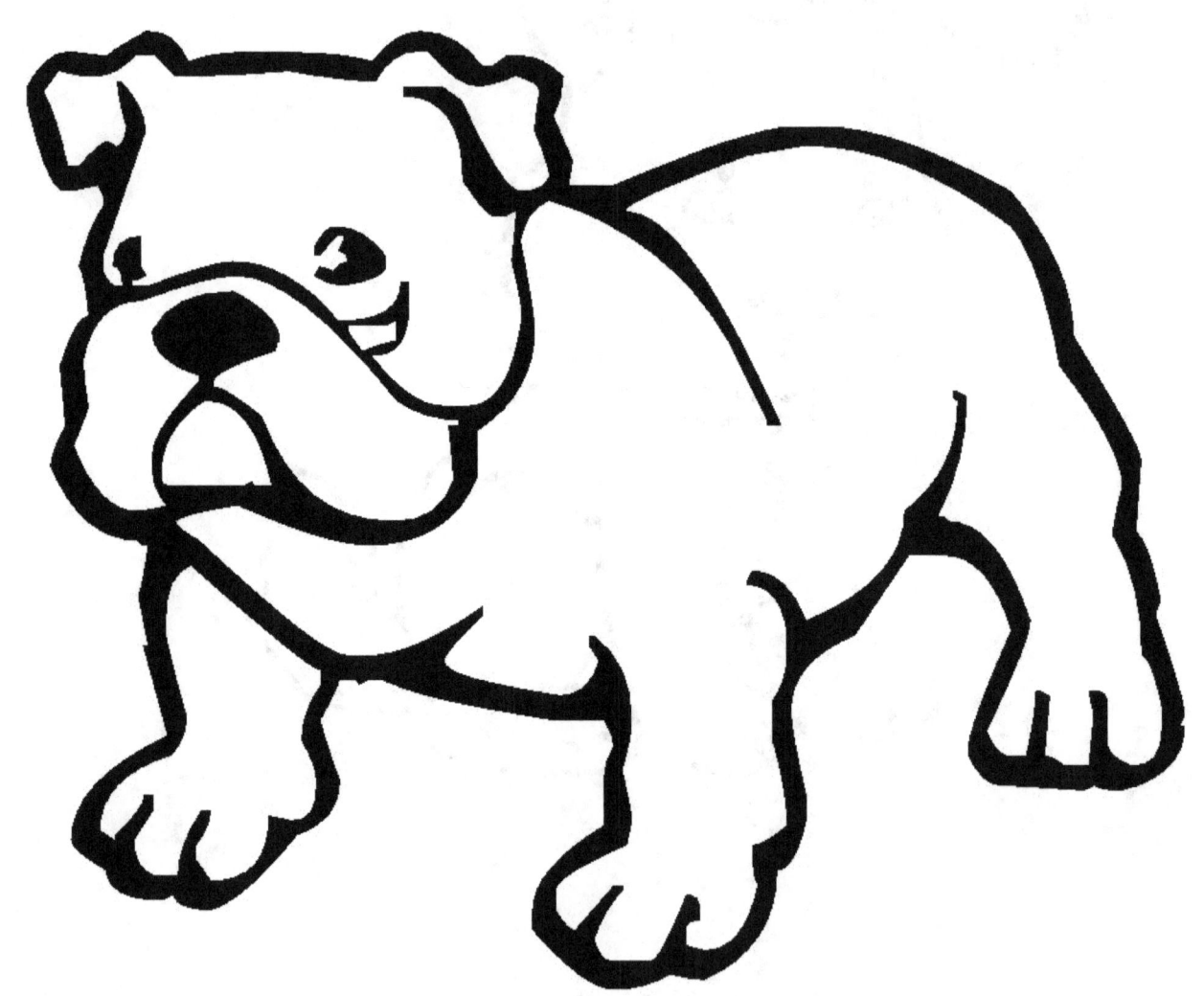

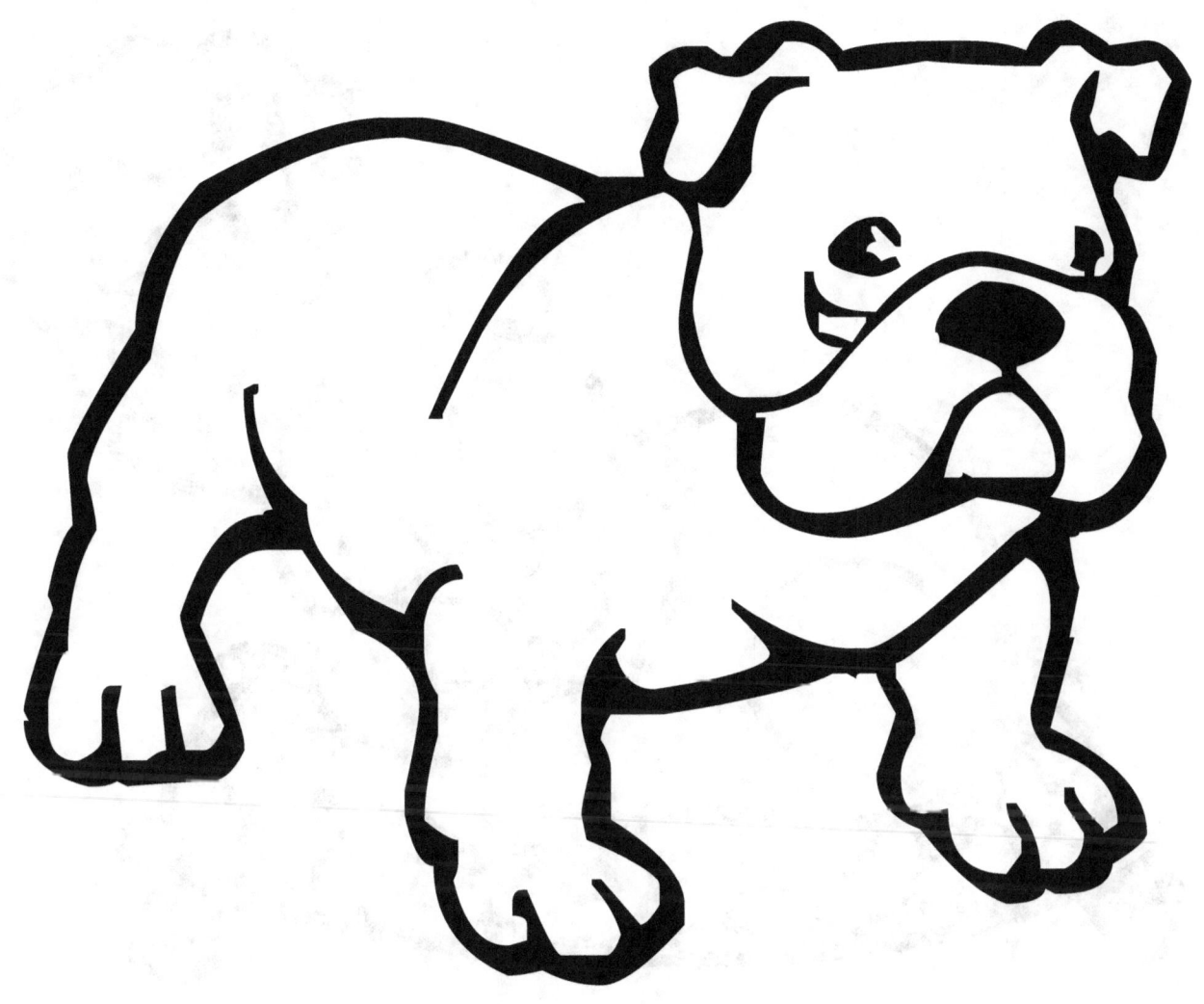

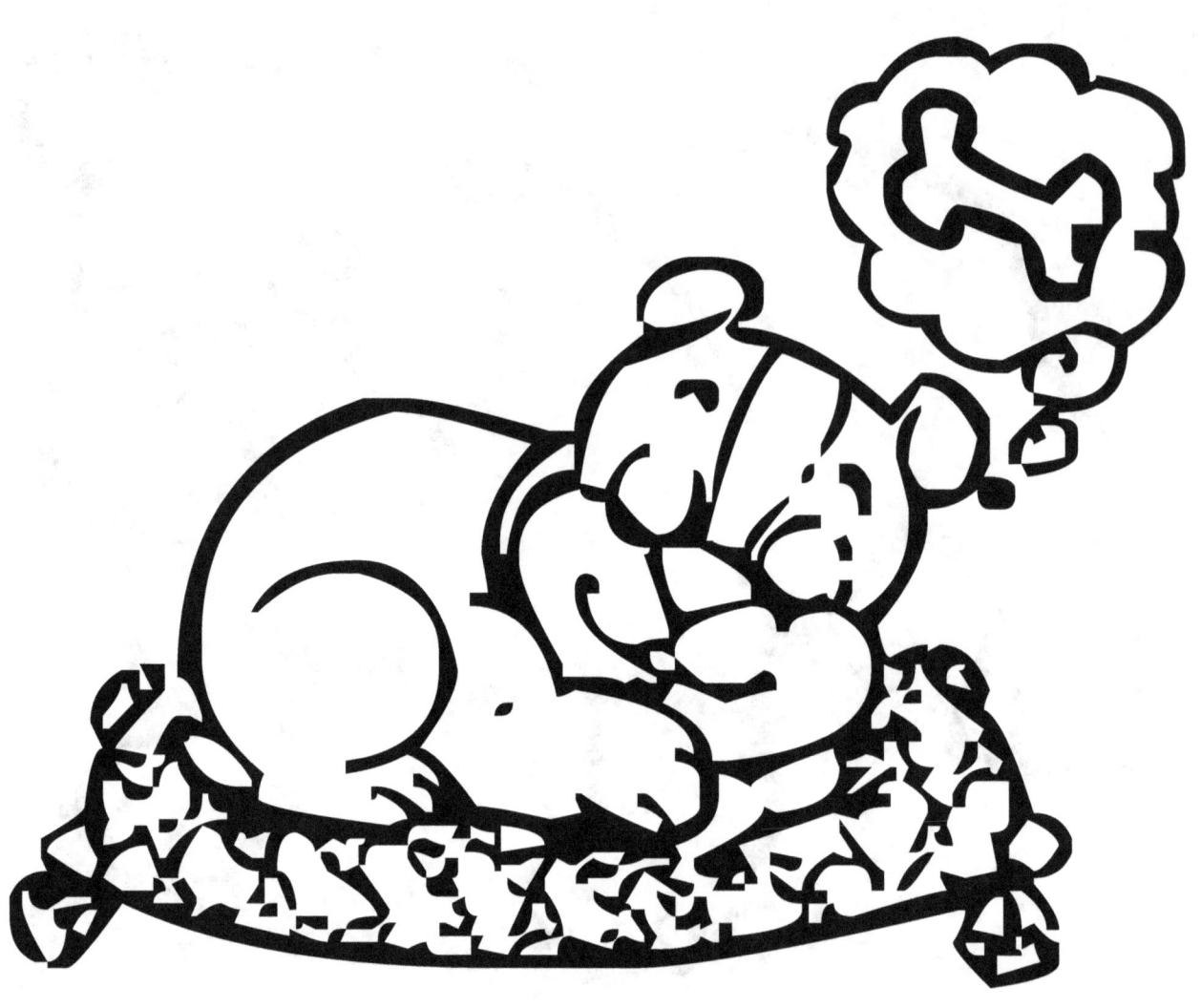

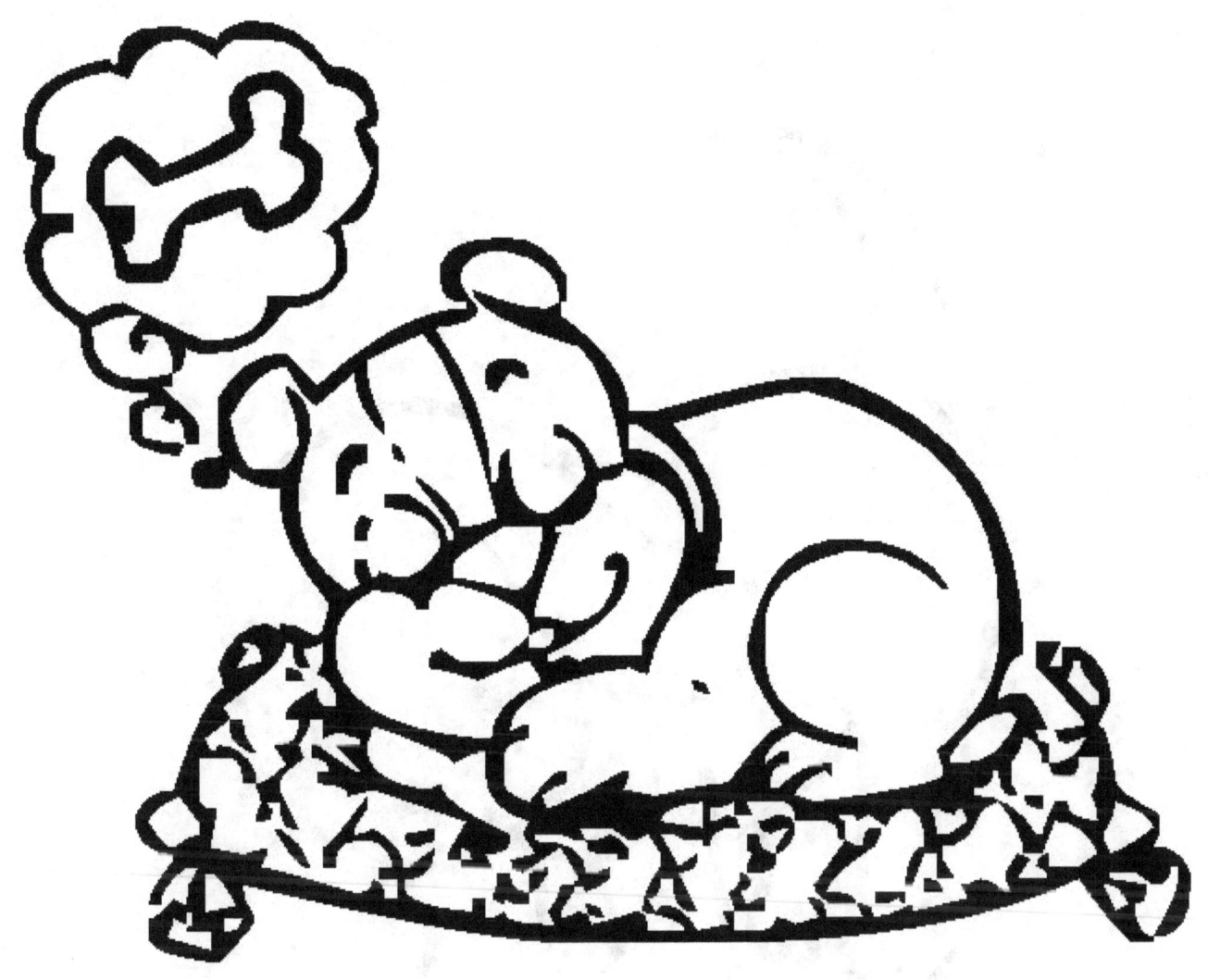

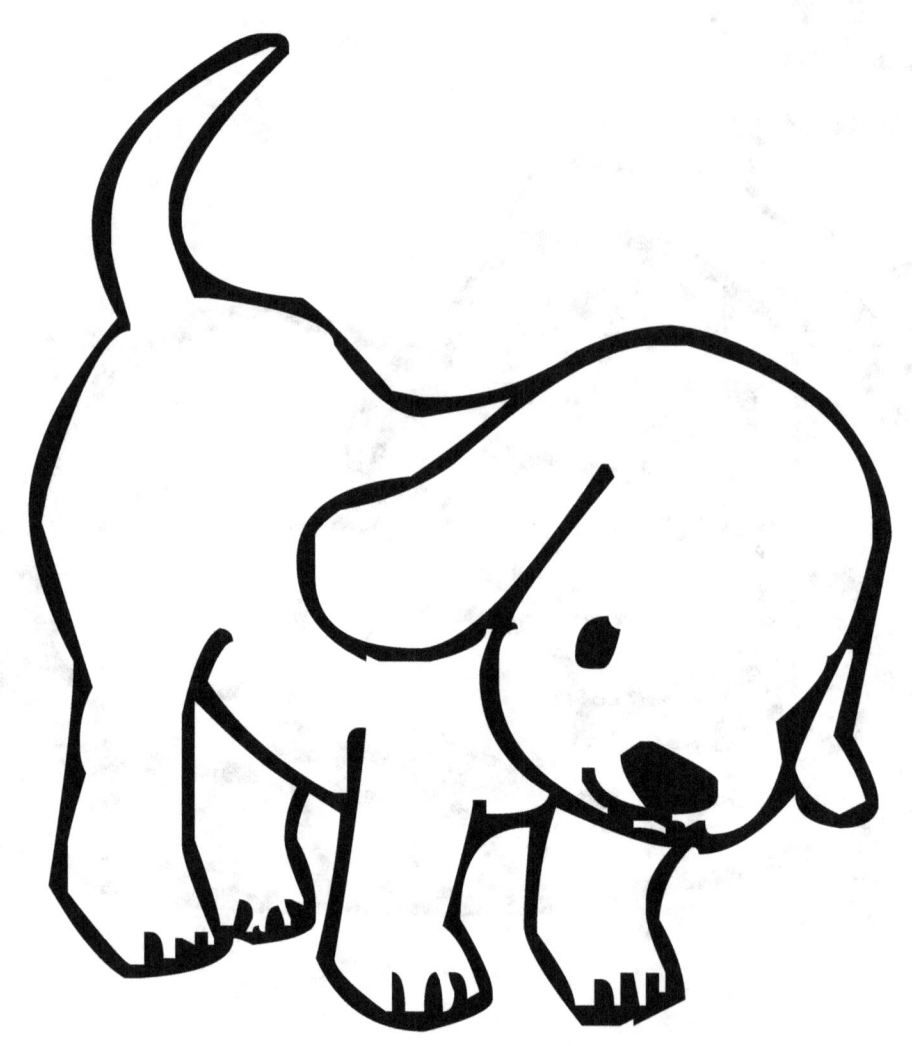

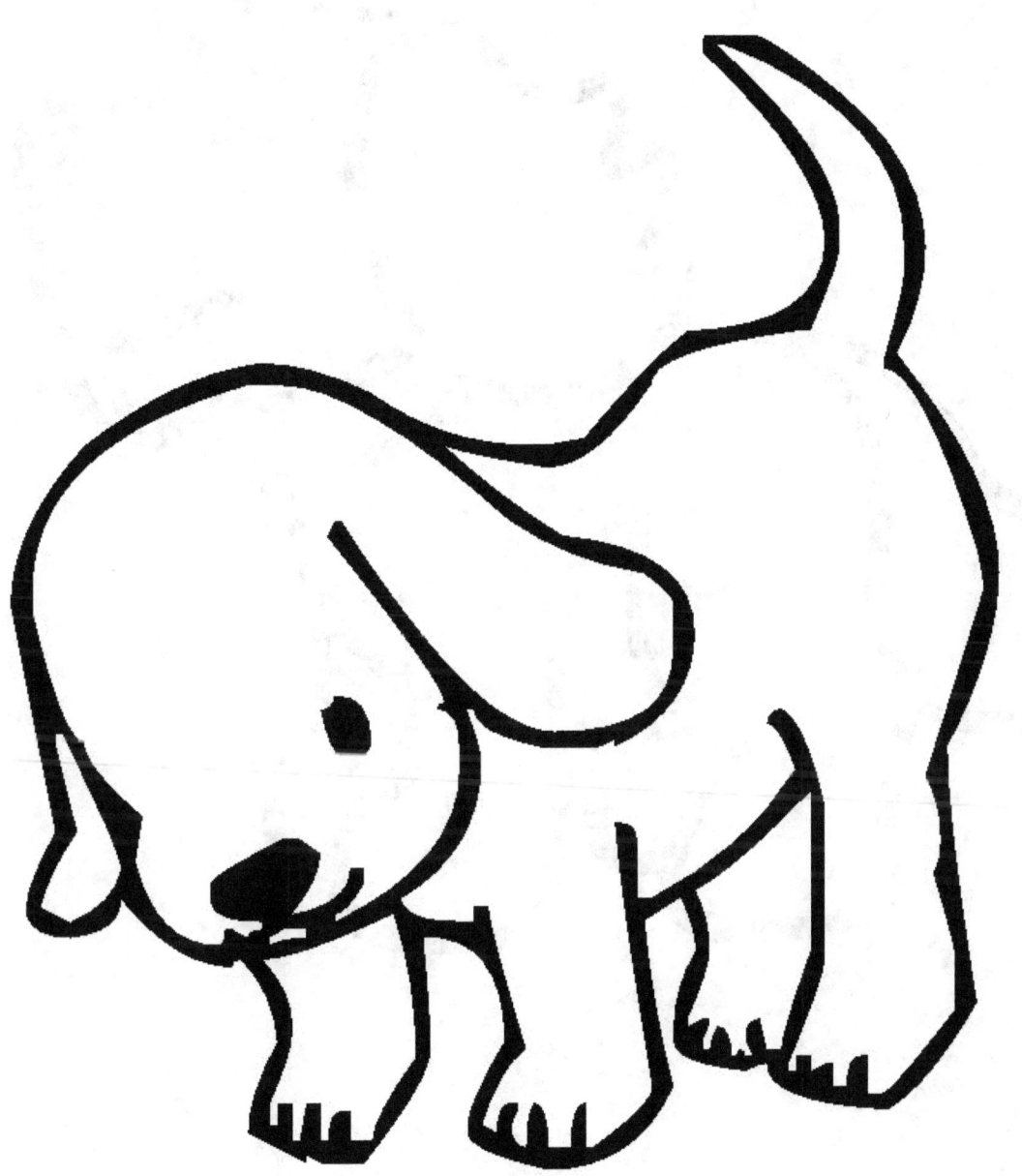

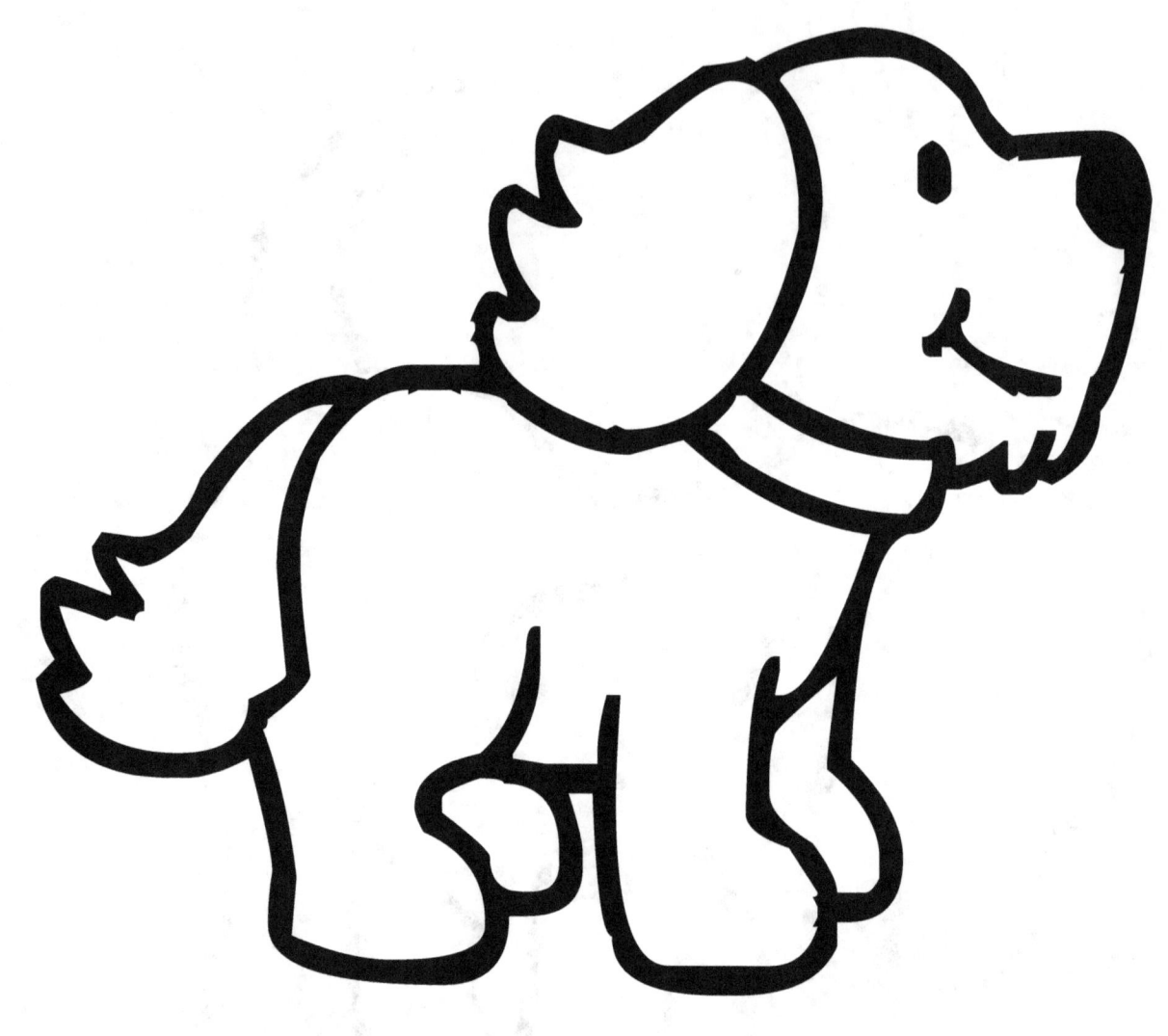

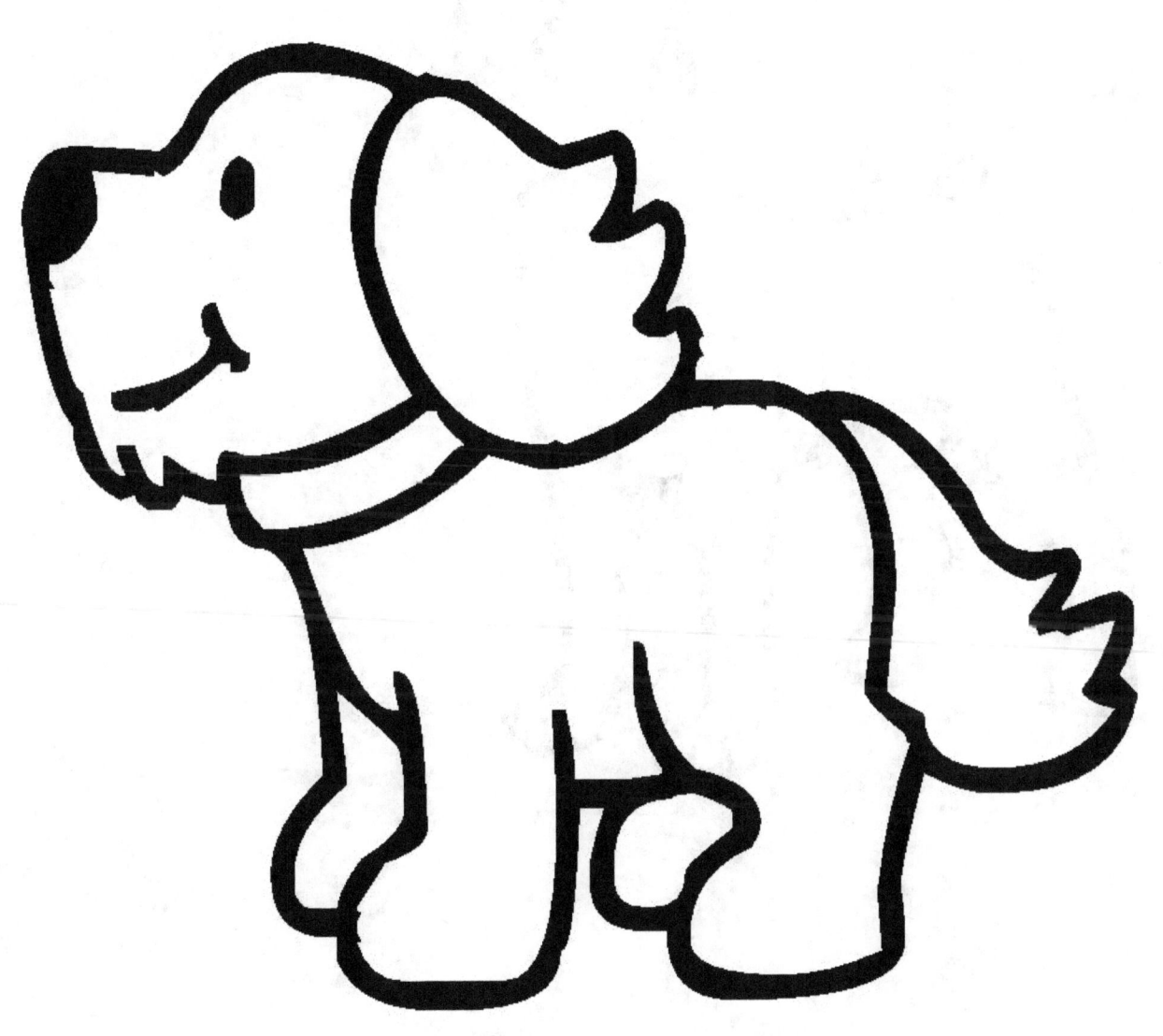

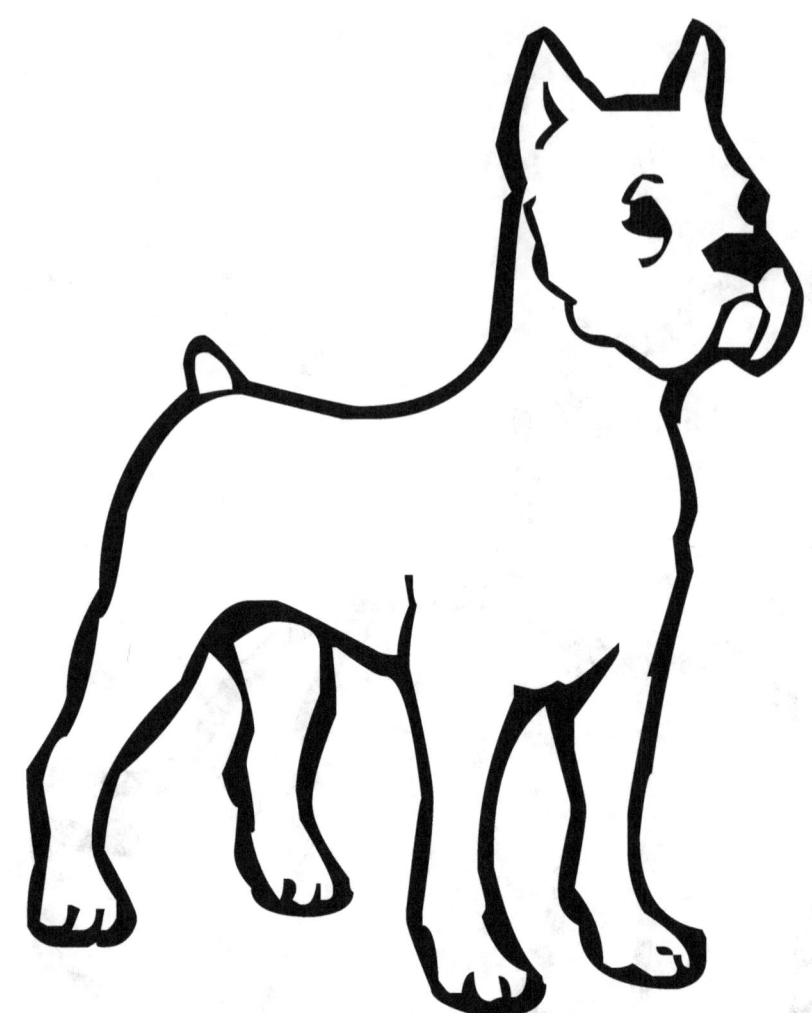

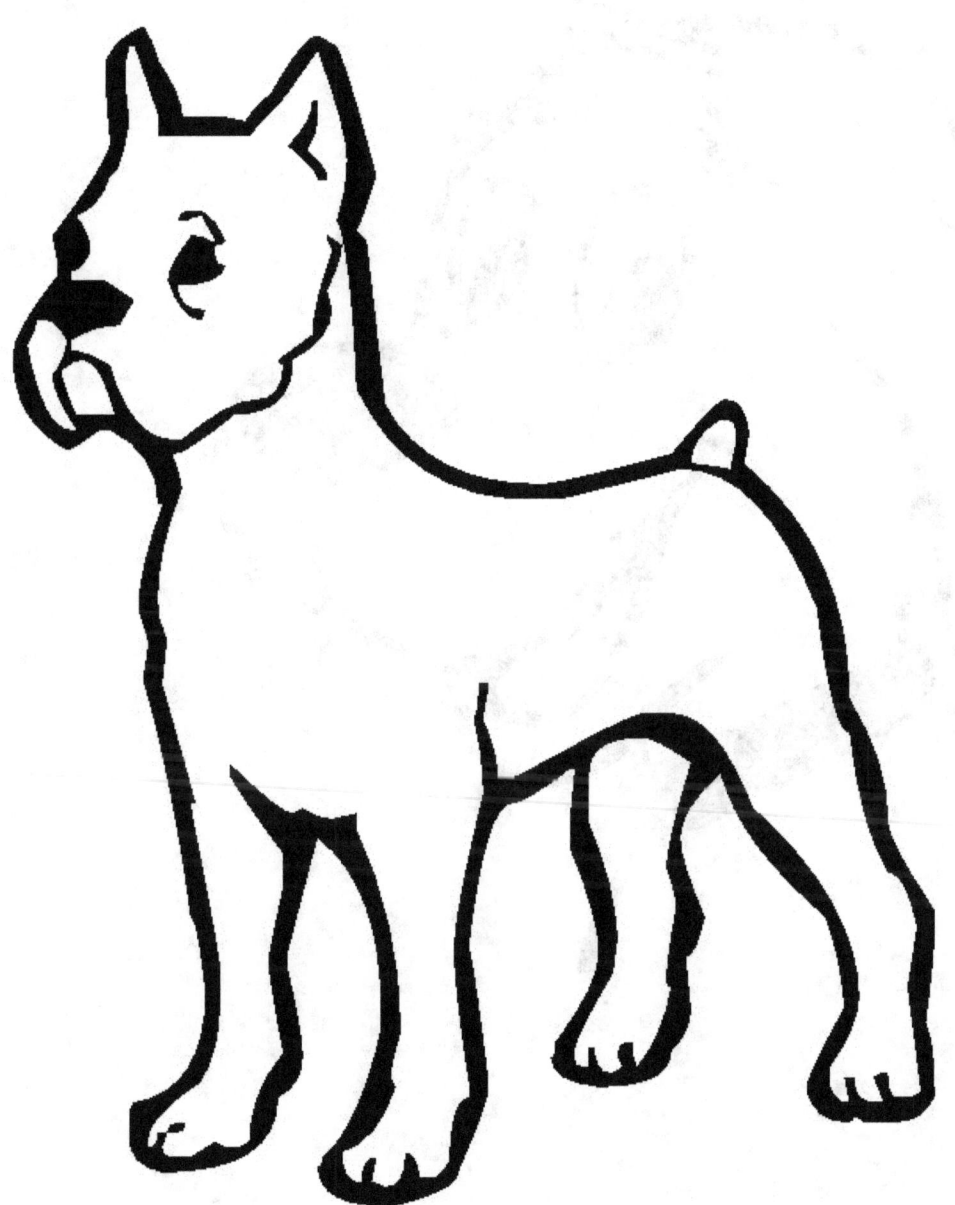

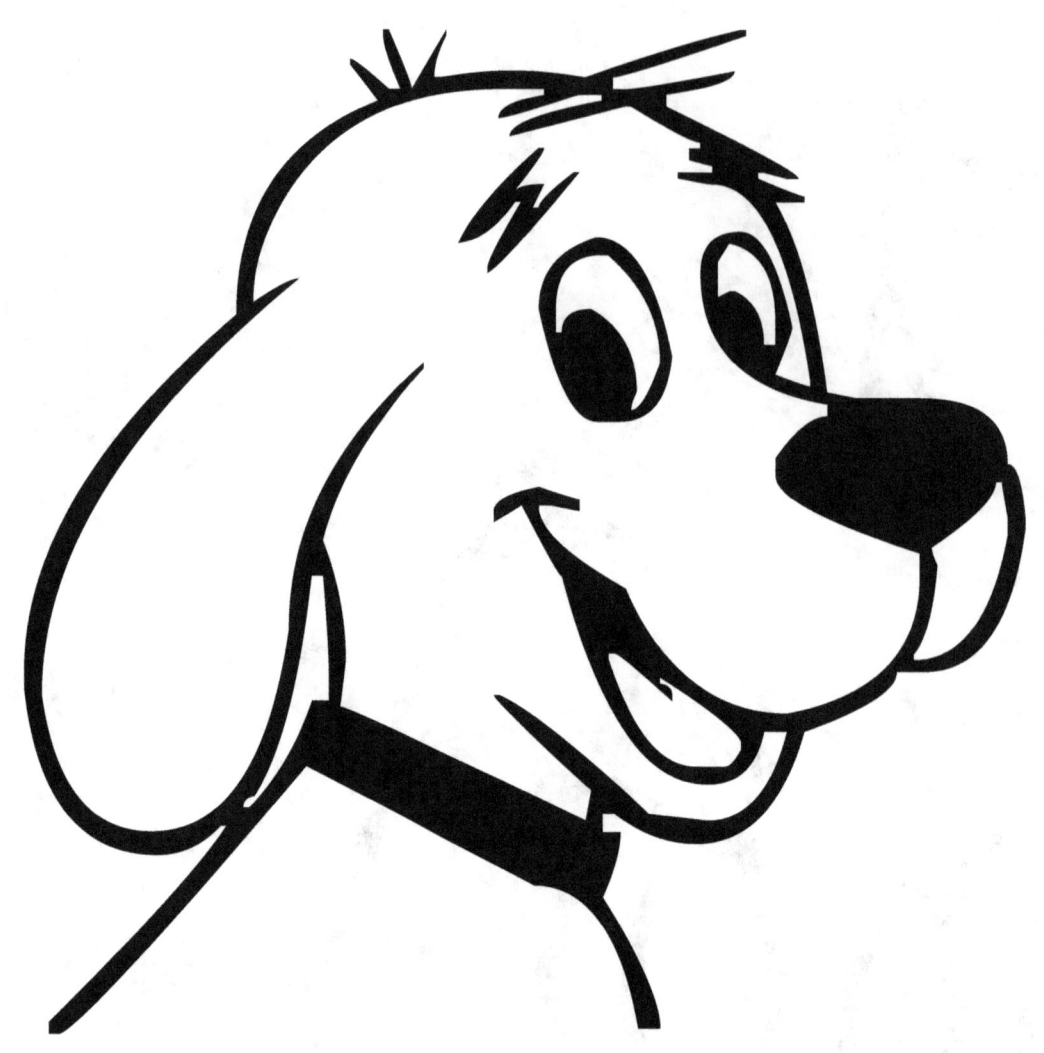

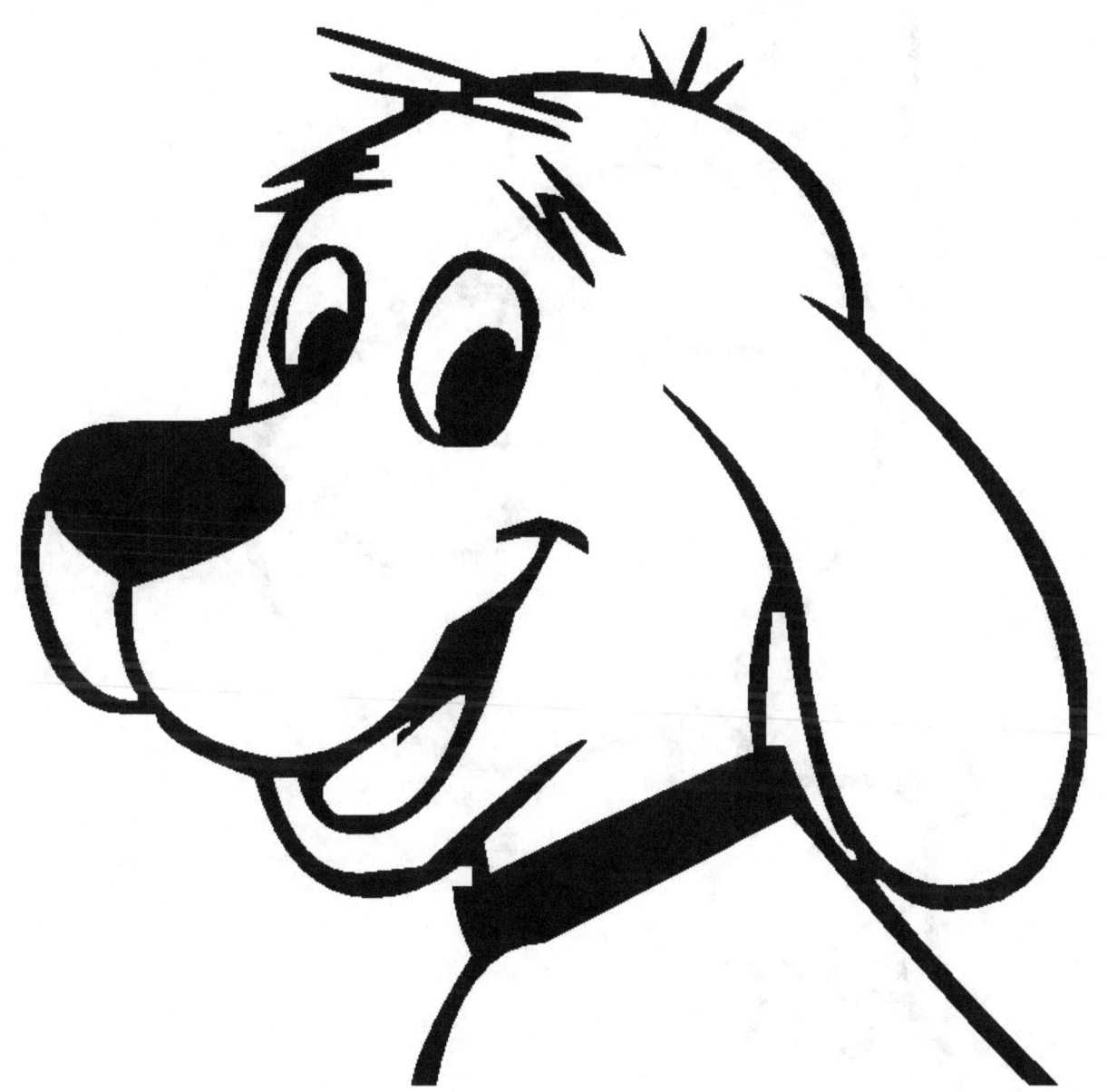

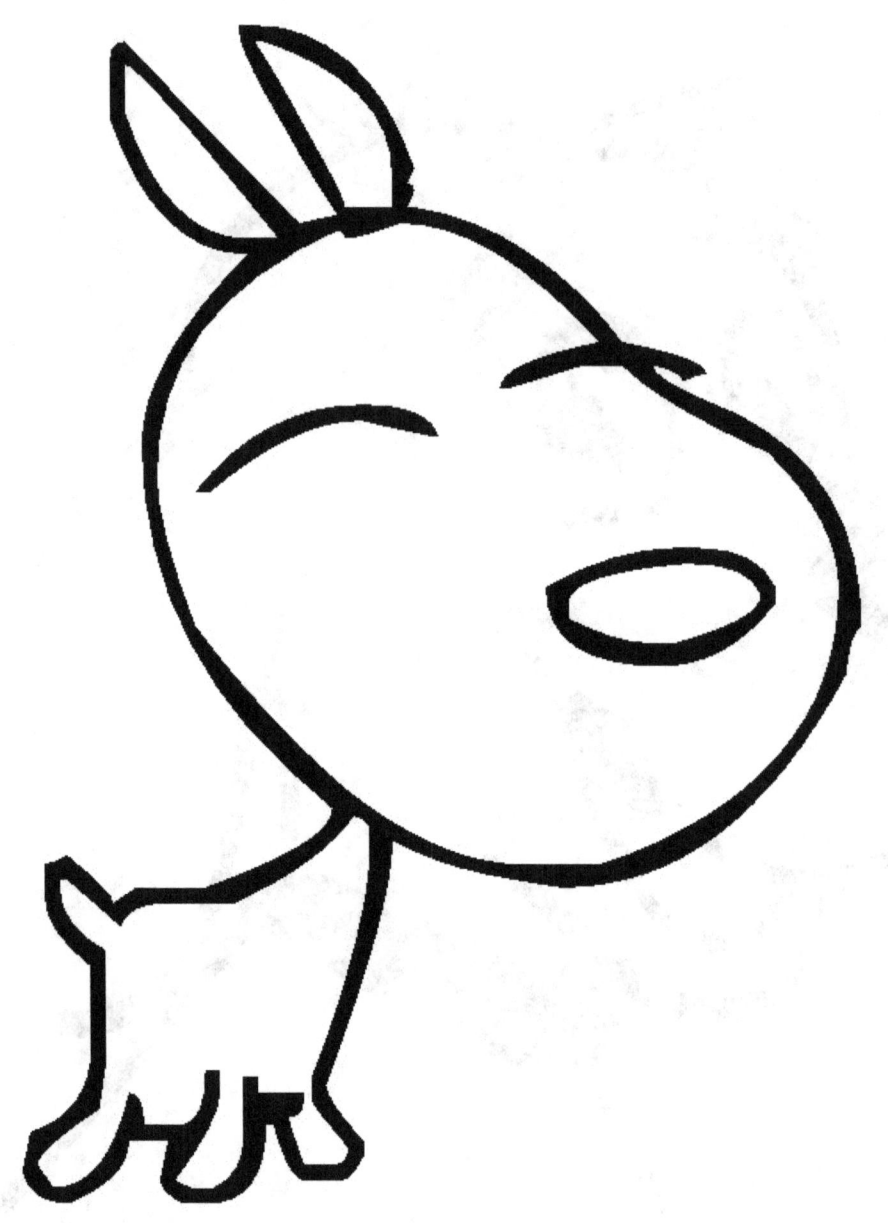

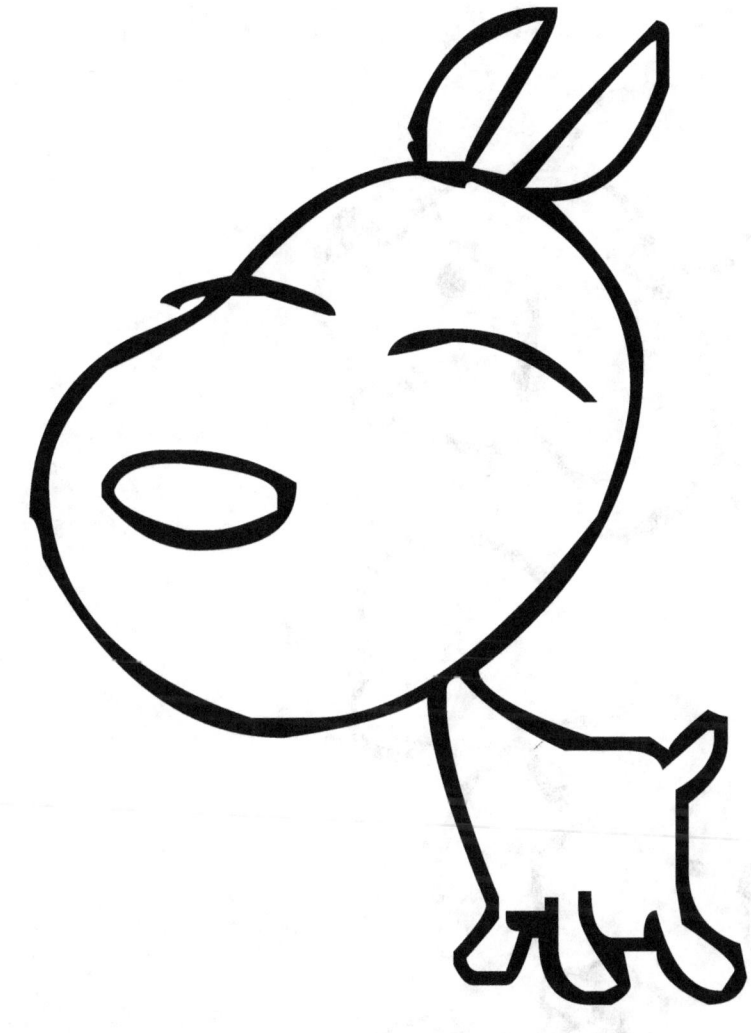

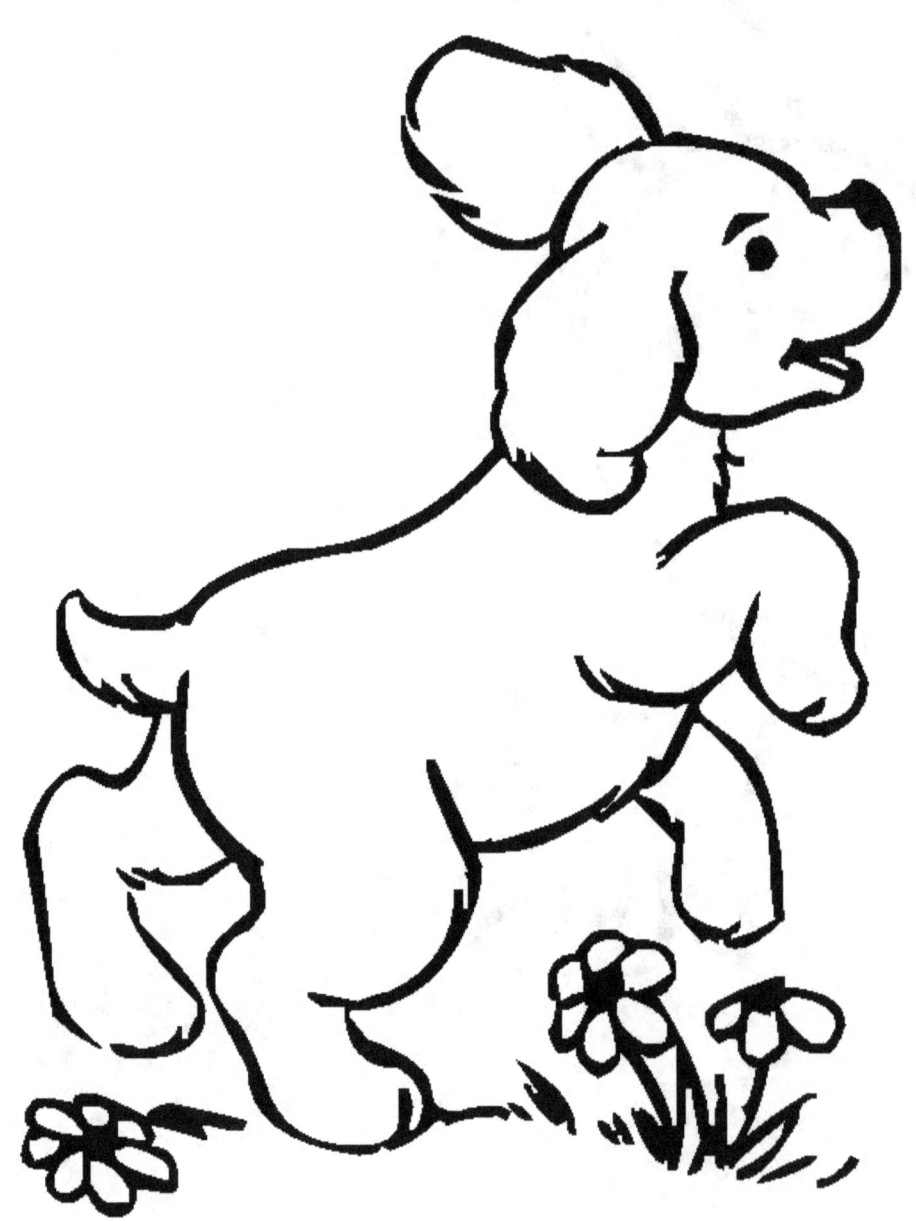

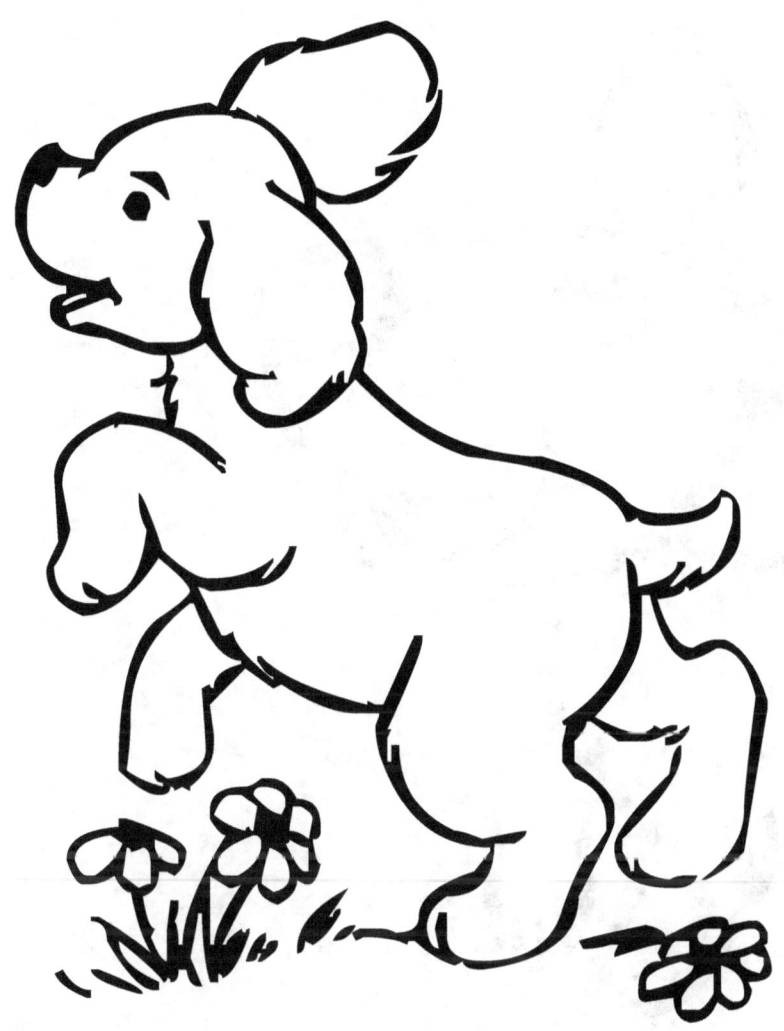

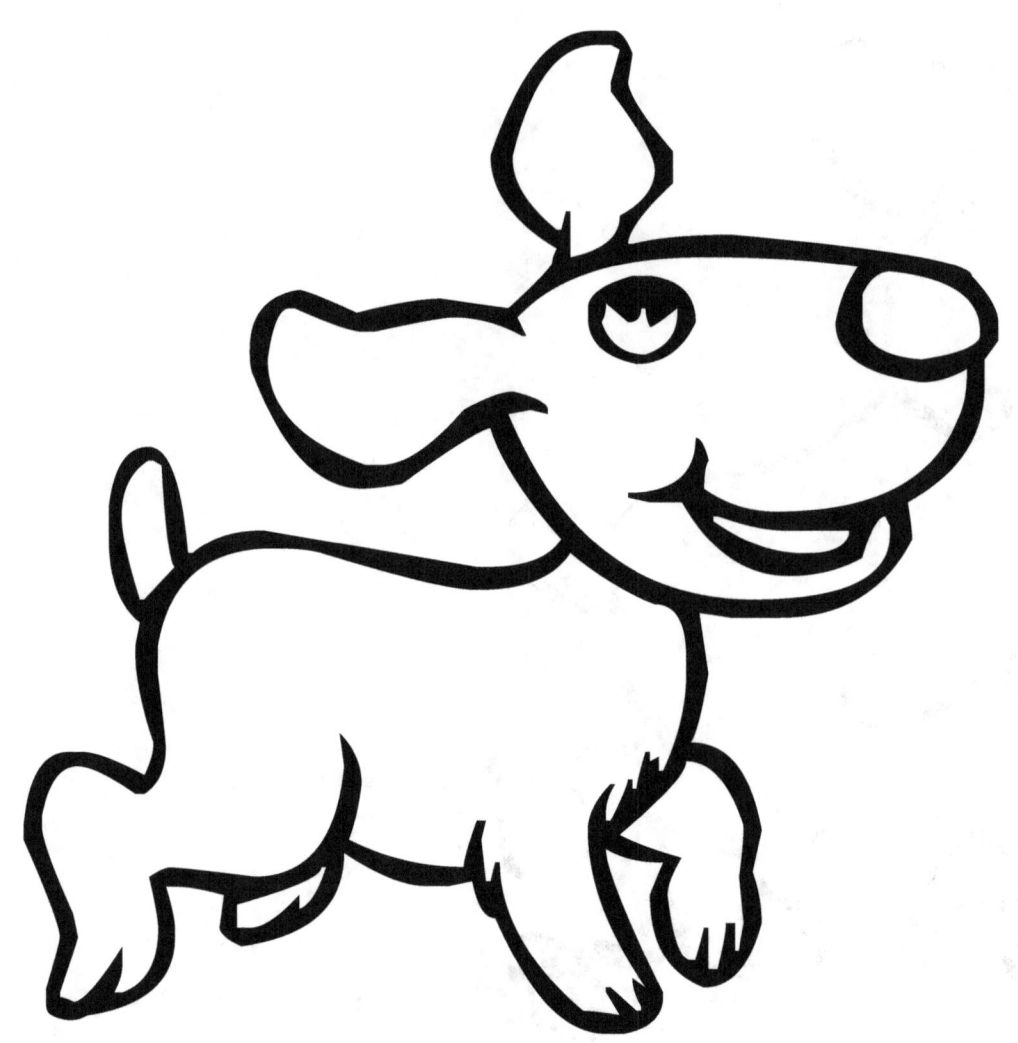

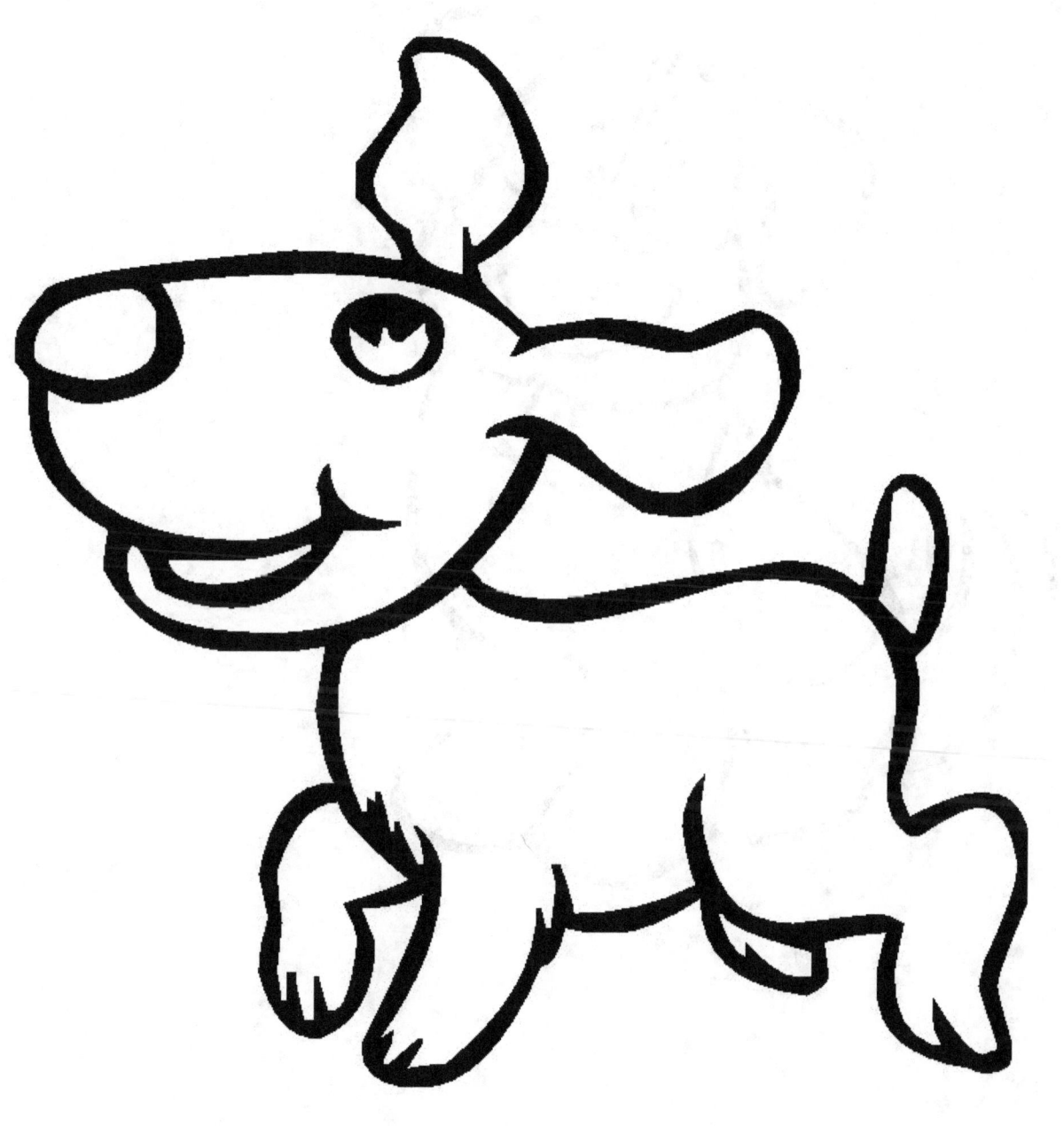

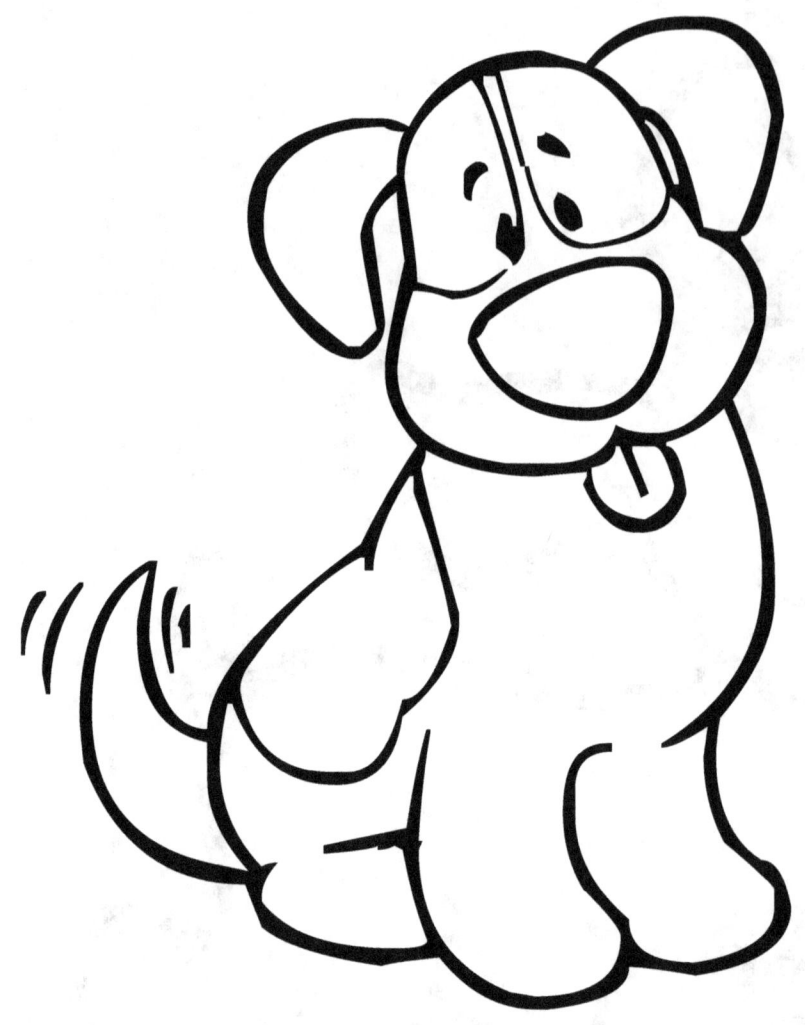

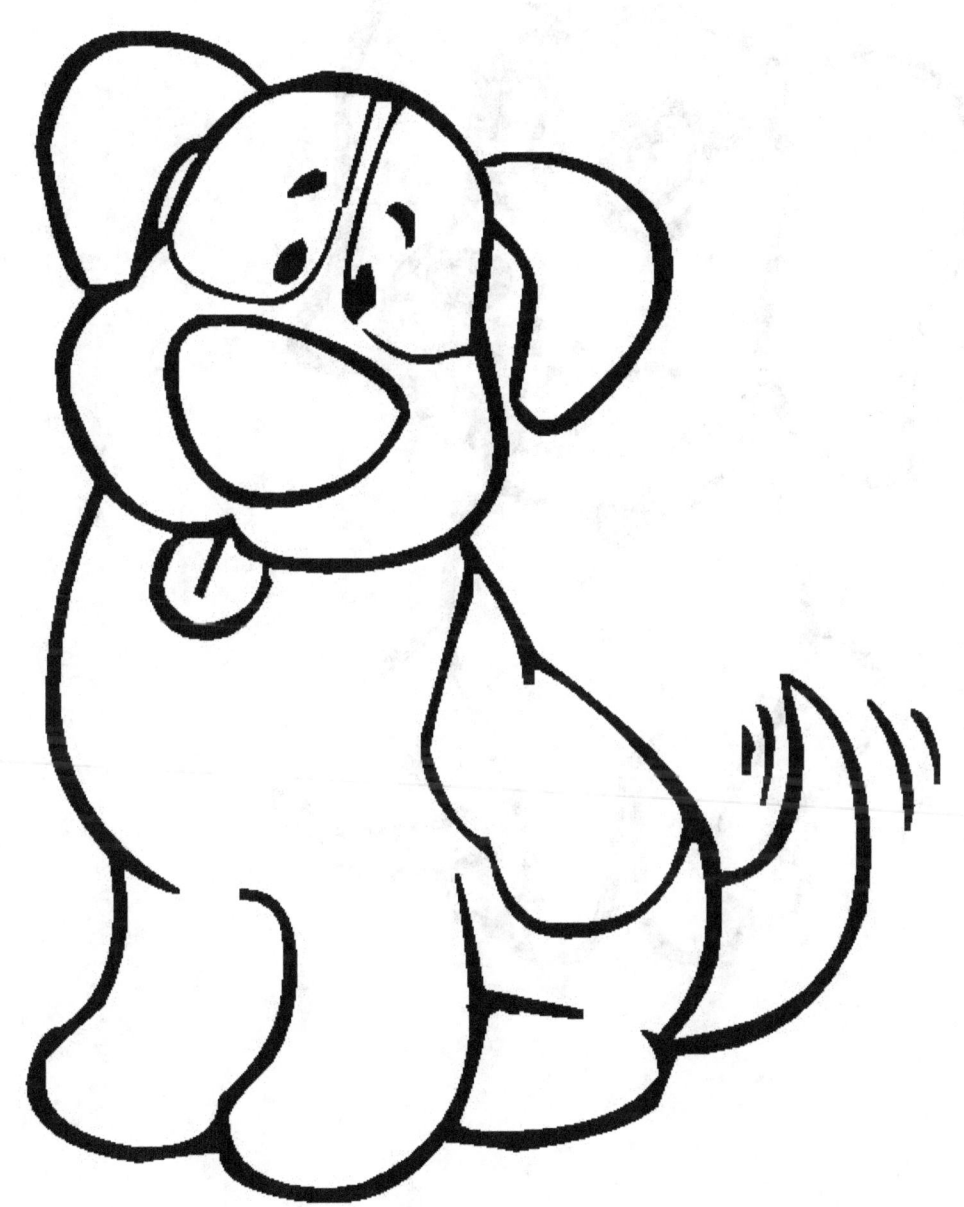

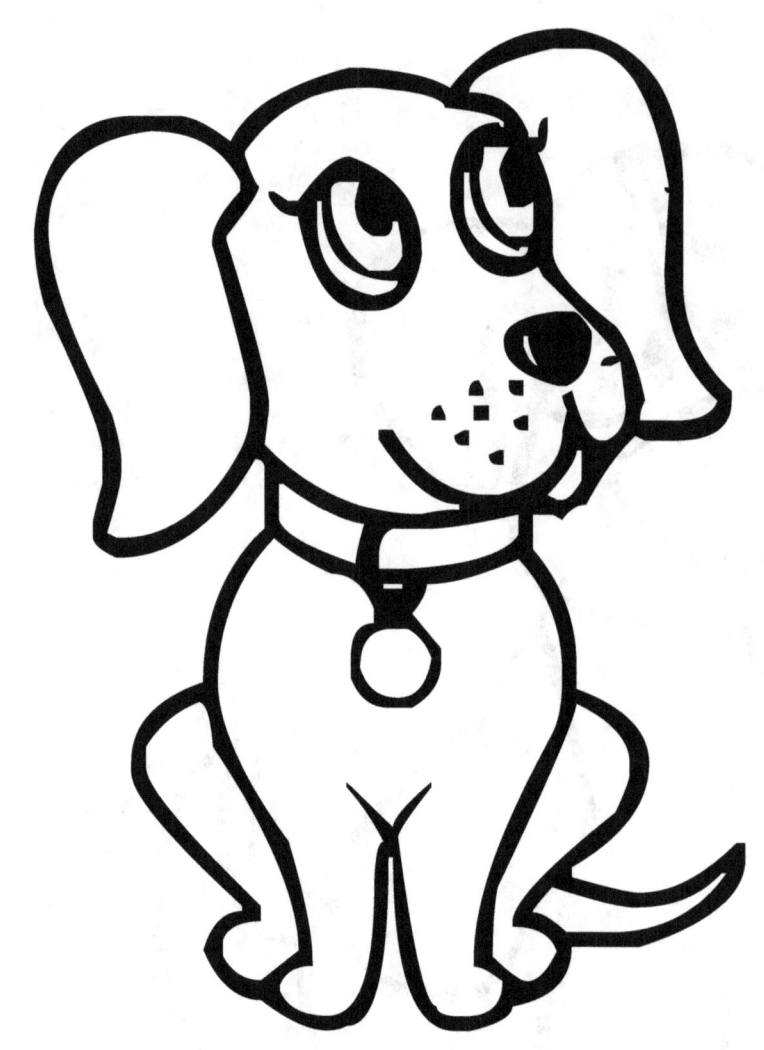

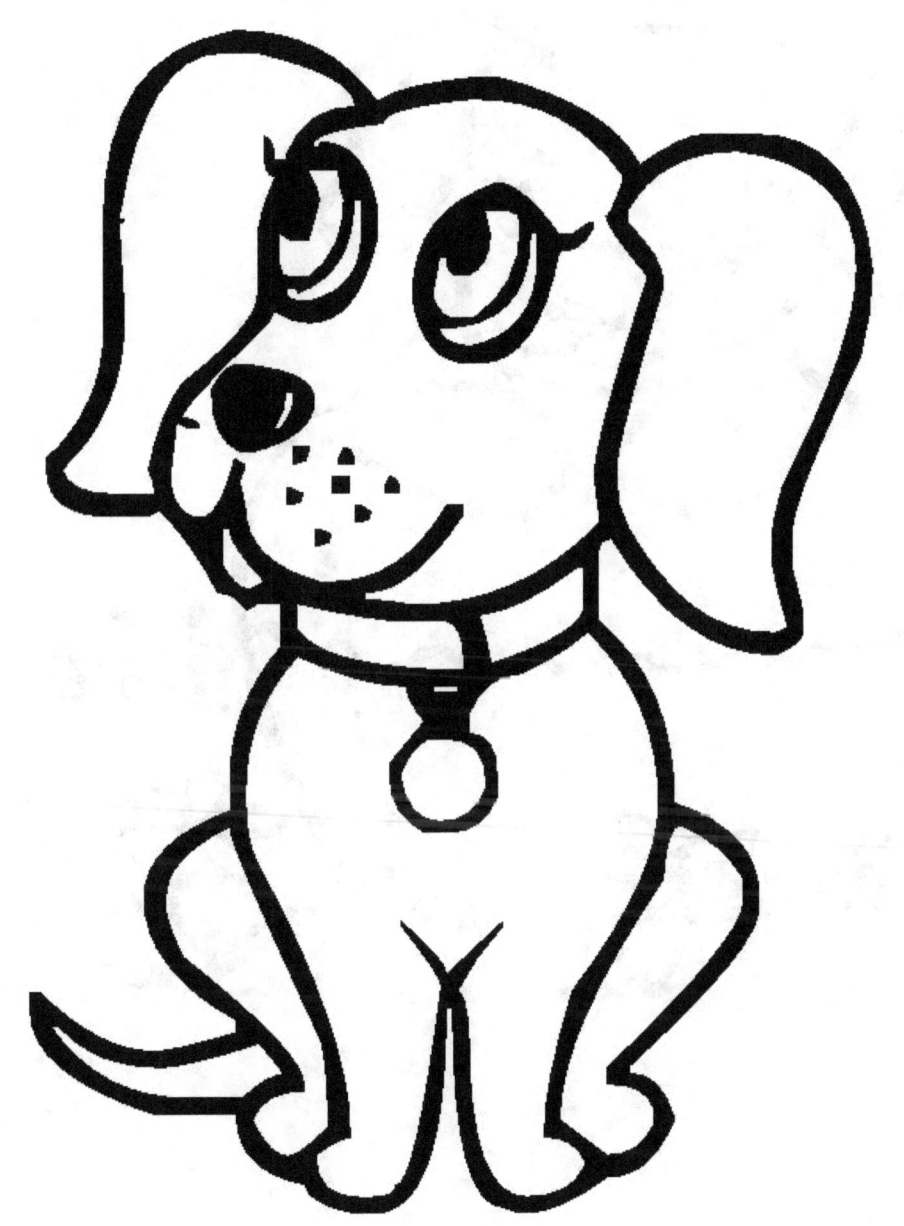

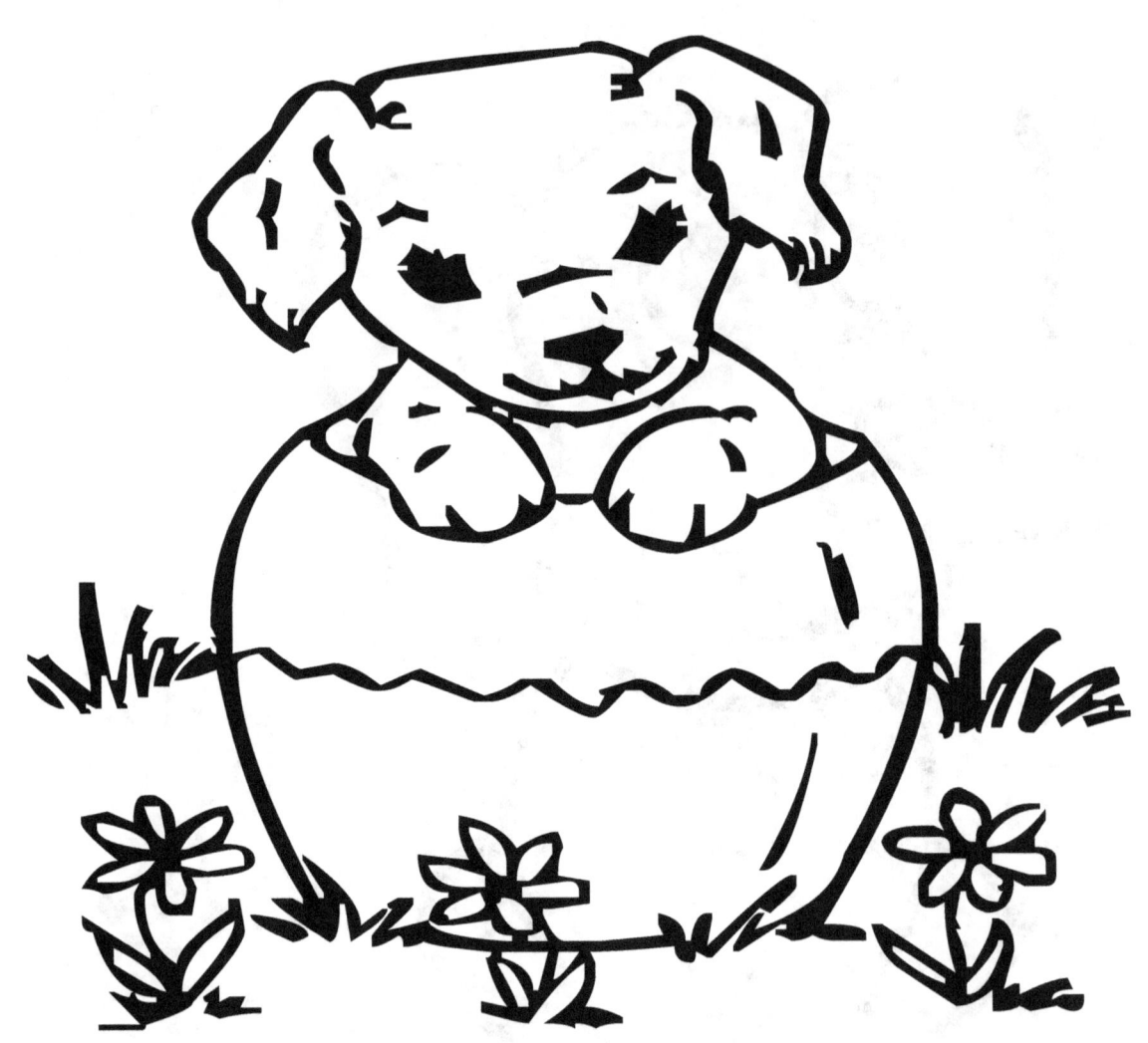

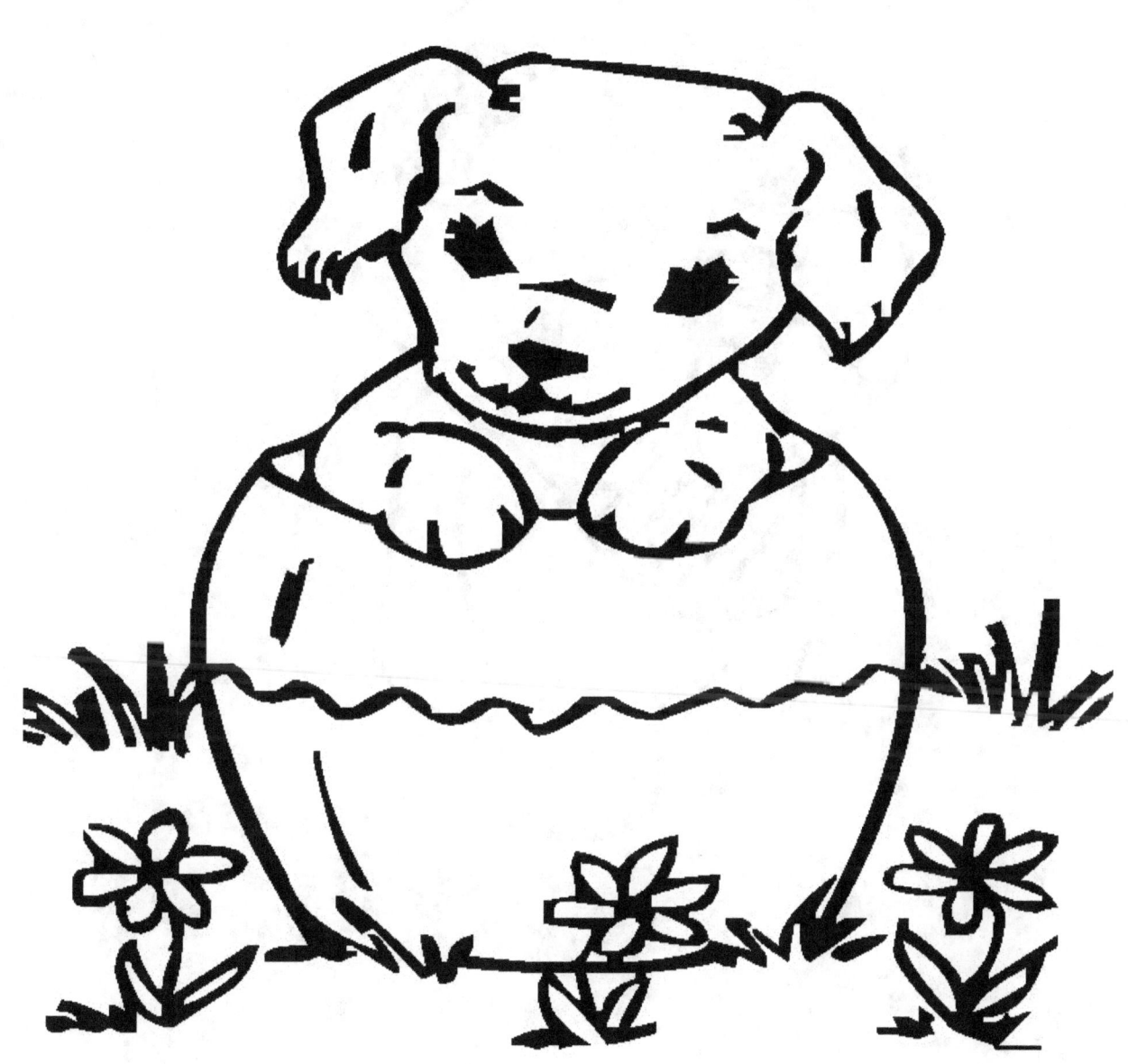

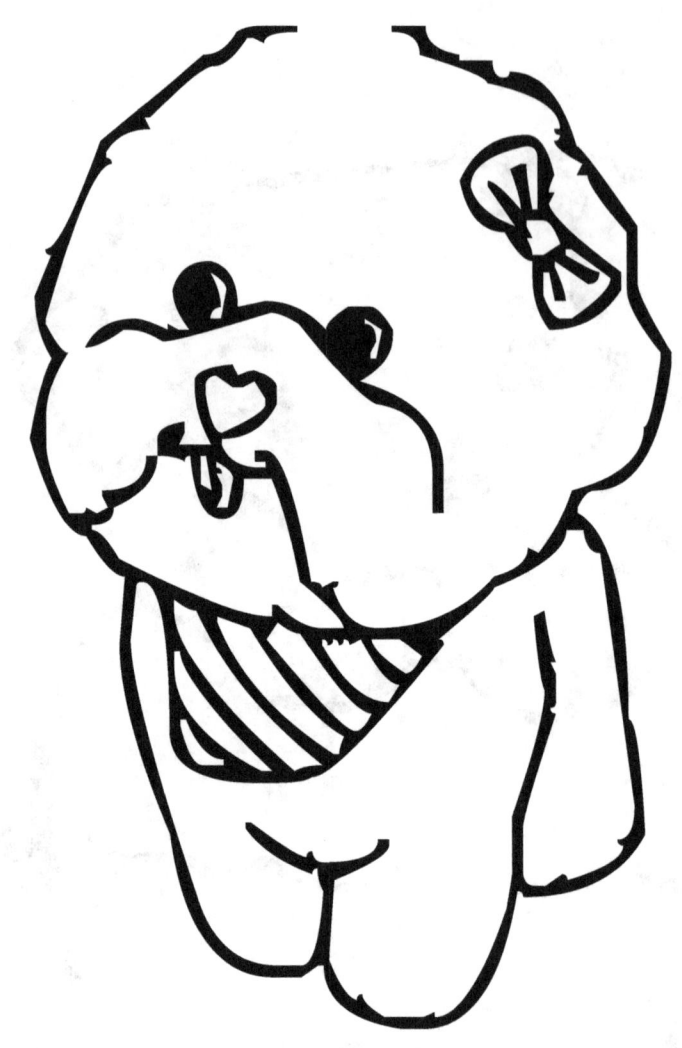

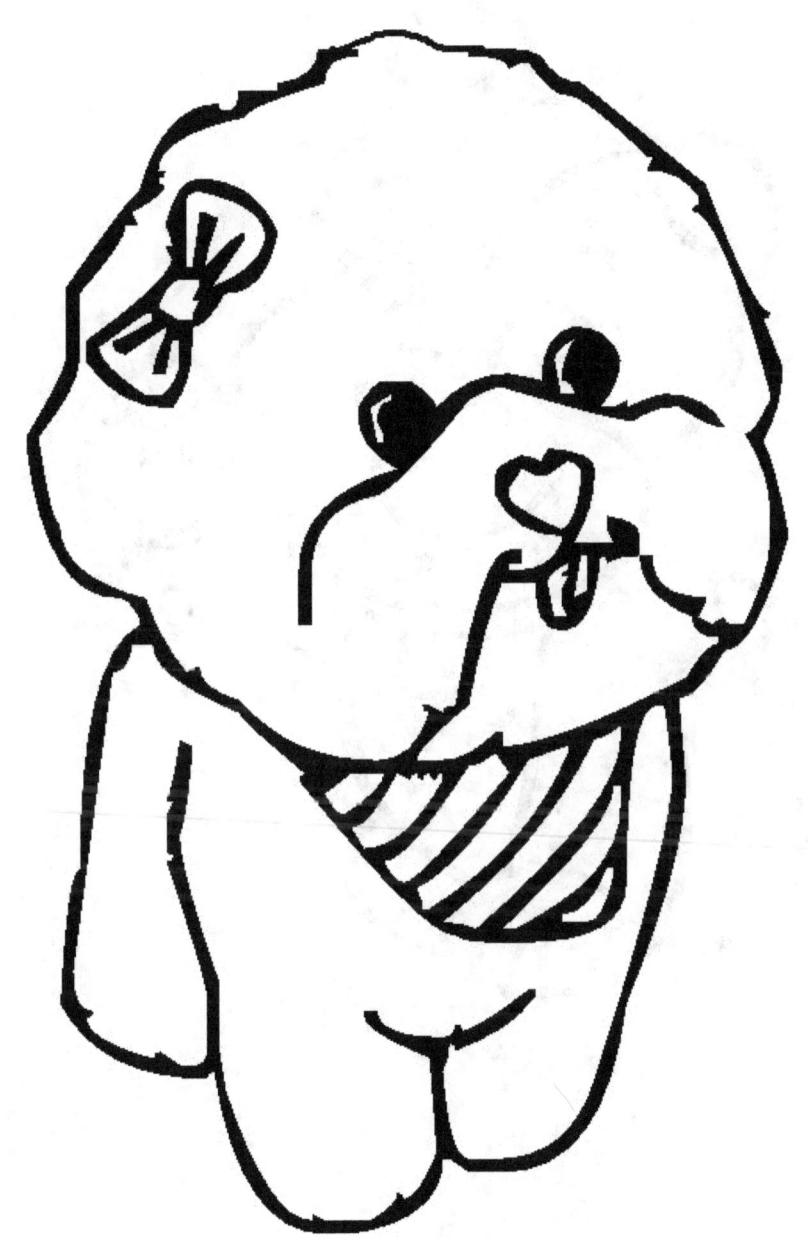

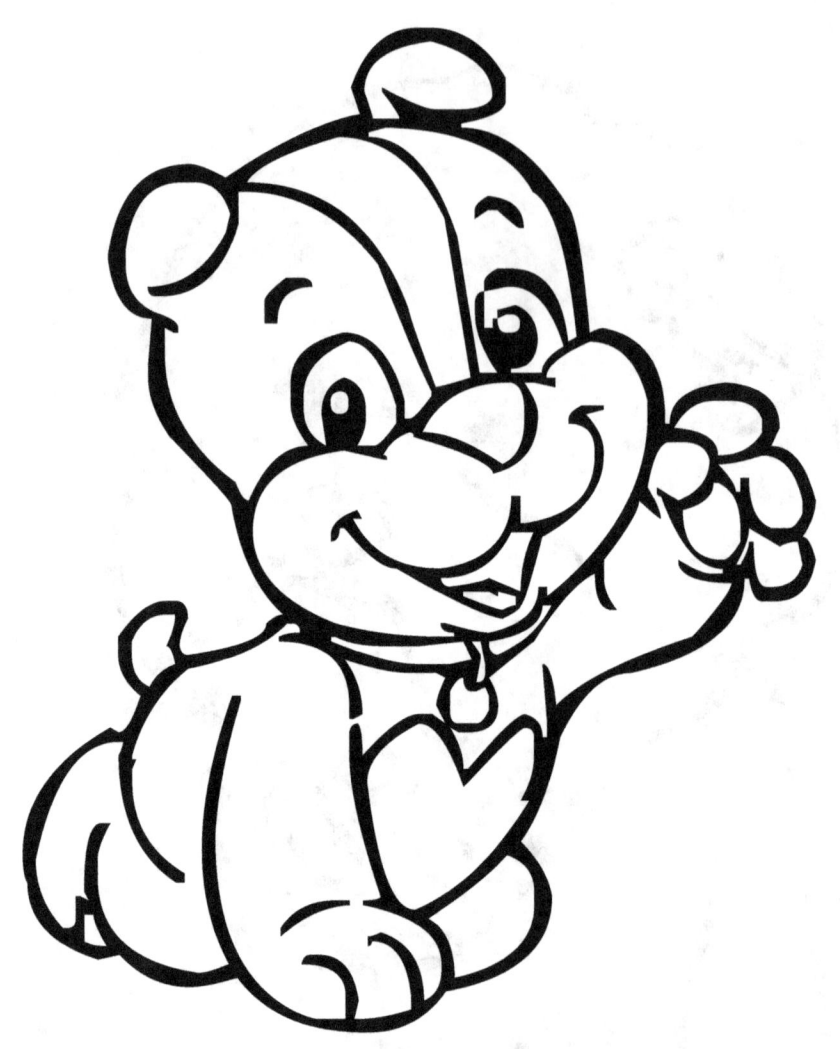

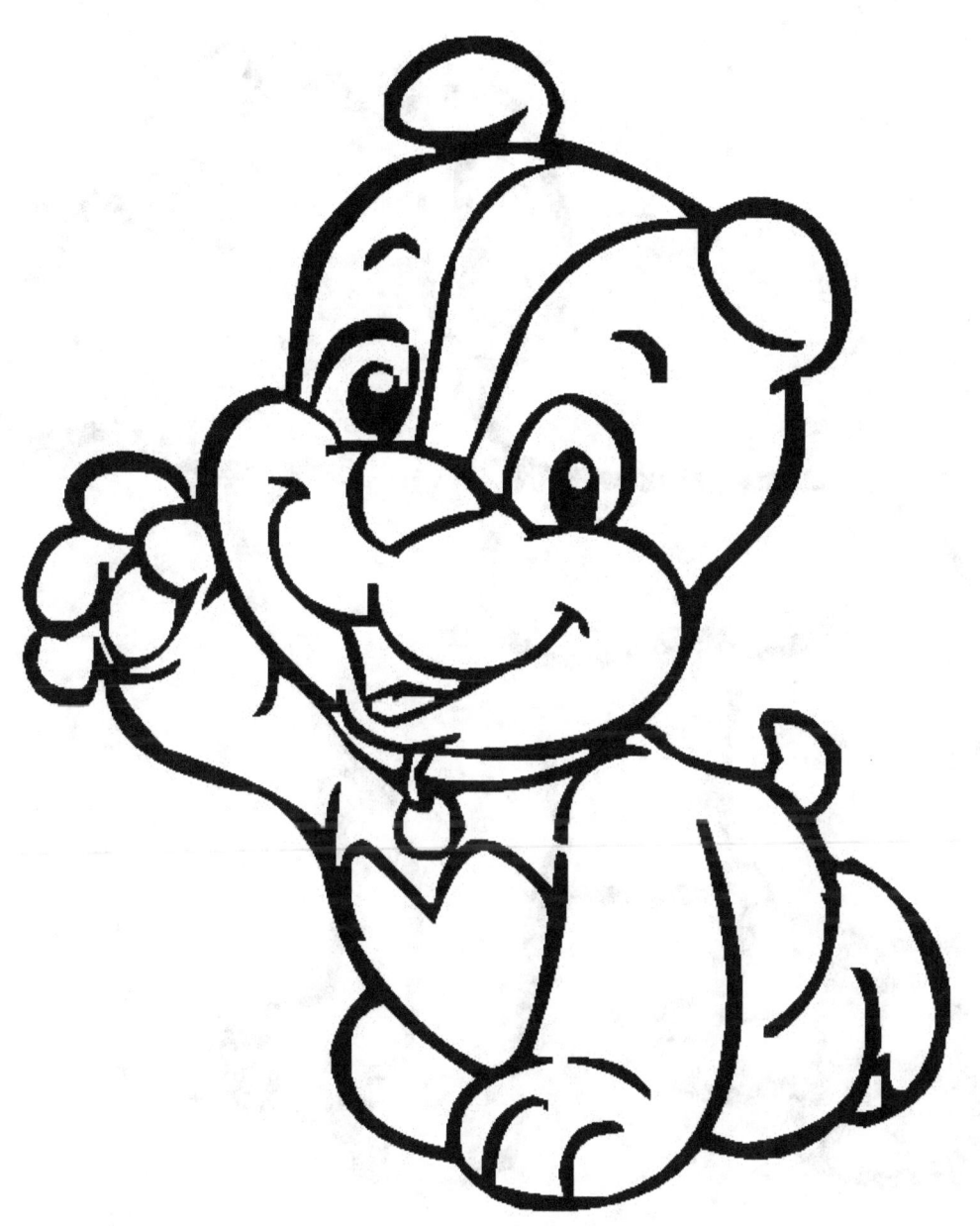

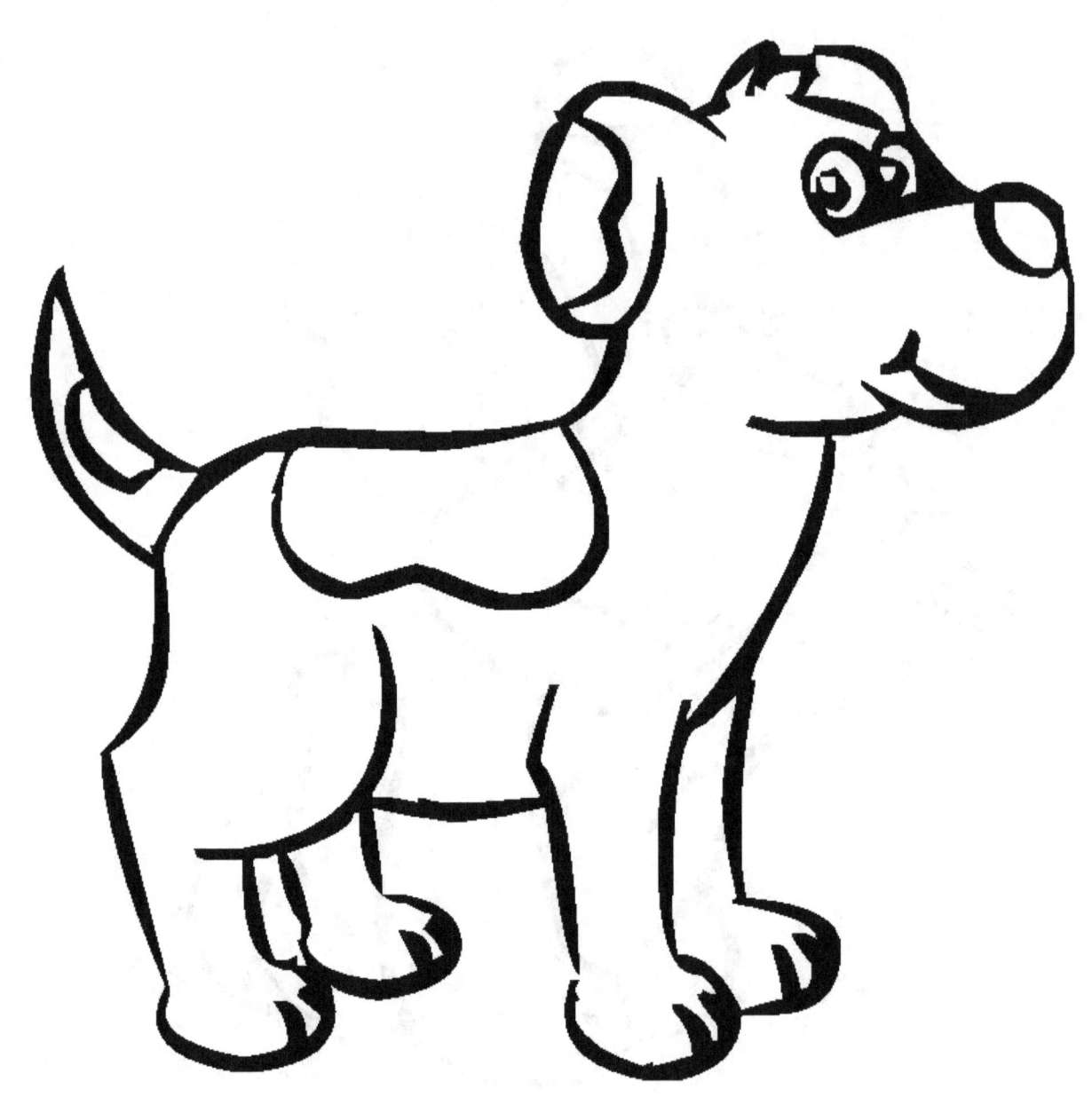

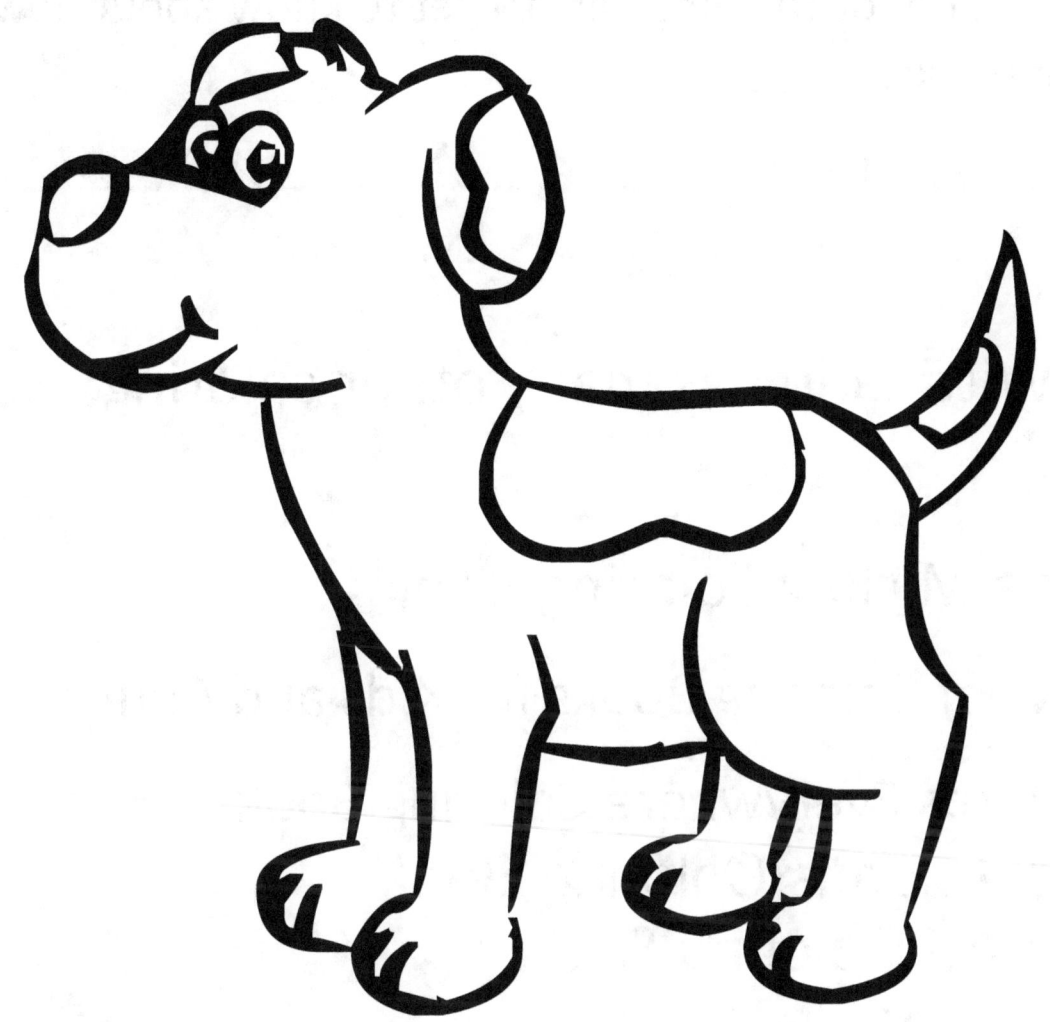

Thank you for buying this coloring book.

Please sign up for the email list to get to know about new coloring books:

www.getspecialbonus.com/coloringbooks/

Gary Wittmann has many other coloring books:

Vintage Mickey Coloring Book

30 Days of Coloring Books for Kids and Adults

Birds, Birds Everywhere Coloring Book
Animal Friends Coloring Book
Easter Art Coloring Book

Visit Gary Wittmann website:

www.garywittmann.com

If you color a page and like it to be put on Facebook:

1. Tell me your first name only.
2. Scan your picture or have your parents to take a picture of you with your picture. (I will put it up on the Facebook page called:
   https://www.facebook.com/30DaysofColoringBooksForKidsandAdults/
3. Don't forget the sign up for newsletters of new fun books.
   www.getspecialbonus.com/coloringbooks/
4. Send your picture to me or ask any questions.
   successfulimagination@gmail.com

Thank you so much,

Gary Wittmann